ENDORSEMENTS

Want to know how to stand for God and share His hope with our generation? Here's your handbook!

Rebecca St. James

It is rare to find a book so relevant to the needs of today and that so exposes the attack of the enemy on minds and hearts. The synthesis of passion and wisdom is not just inspiring, but altogether applicable to modern life. The urgency to rise up and preach a Gospel that is relevant to our times reaches out from the pages and grabs a hold of your heart. We encourage everyone to digest this book. Let us fight for our friends! Let us fight for our souls!

Korey Cooper, Guitar/ Keyboards—Skillet

In *Battle Cry for My Generation*, Ron Luce has uncovered the subtle plan of the enemy through an educated look at the trends and statistics of today's pop-culture. The war is raging, and this book is a wake-up call to a generation of souls who are on the front lines whether they realize it or not.

Jason Morant

I have had the honor of being a part of Teen Mania's ministry for over five years now, and I have personally seen the impact they are having in the lives of youth and adults in our country. It's been so exciting and encouraging to see the passion that Ron Luce has for this country and this world. Reading this book ignited my passion to be a part of this army! It challenged me never to grow complacent but to keep training. We are each called every day to be heroes in our lives, in the small and the huge choices we make. We are to fight for what's right. I see so many lives ruined and affected by this war, people I love, people I feel helpless to save, and people who need someone to fight for them when their strength is gone.

Tricia Brock, Superchic[k]

Battle Cry for My Generation helps us to take a painfully honest look in the mirror to care like Jesus does in our generation.

Michael Gungor

Many of those in leadership positions are trying to reach this 21st century generation with 20th century methods. They are simply out of touch with the generation they are called to impact. While many leaders lack the ability to relate, Ron Luce shows us how to reach, relate to, and revolutionize this generation with *Battle Cry*.

L.G. Wise, Rap Artist/Speaker

RON LUCE
WITH MIKE GUZZARDO

NexGen® is an imprint of
Cook Communications Ministries
Colorado Springs, CO 80918
Cook Communications, Paris, Ontario
Kingsway Communications, Eastbourne, England

BATTLE CRY FOR MY GENERATION
© 2006 by Ron Luce

The Word at Work Around the World
A vital part of Cook Communications Ministries is our international
outreach, Cook Communications International (CCMI). Your purchase of
this book, and of other books and Christian-growth products from Cook,
enables CCMI to provide Bibles and Christian literature to people in more
than 150 languages in 65 countries.

Cover Design: Big Mouth Bass Design
Interior Design: Sandy Flewelling, TrueBlue Design
Interior Photos: © by Stockbyte (unless otherwise noted)

First Printing, 2006
Printed in the United States of America
        3 4 5 6 7 8 9 10 11 Printing/Year 12 11 10 09 08 07 06

Library of Congress Control Number: 2005938077
ISBN-10: 0-7814-4379-2
ISBN-13: 978-0-7814-4379-1

CONTENTS

intro

One of the most famous battles in the history of the world was the Allied invasion of Normandy during World War II. The D-Day attack on that bloody beach turned the entire tide of the war. The few Nazis who survived said they could not believe the tenacity of warriors who landed—the soldiers just kept coming, no matter how much firepower the enemy unleashed.

We're facing a similar, terrifying challenge. Though the battle is spiritual, and sometimes invisible, the attack facing your generation today is not unlike what the Allies were facing in World War II. It took a massive coordinated effort such as D-Day to turn things around and break the enemy's back. In the same way, your war will also take a massive and coordinated effort to rise up against an enemy that sometimes you cannot see—and that sometimes gets right up in your face. But by the power of God and courageous action, it's a war we can win.

the greatest risk is doing nothing

During World War II the Nazis stormed across Europe, destroying communities. They were determined to impose their ideology and values on a passive world. They had conquered virtually every nation they invaded. Even as they threatened England with total domination, they seemed unstoppable—and yet plans were already being laid for a strategic counteroffensive.

The best minds in the free world put nearly two years into planning what became known as the D-Day invasion at Normandy. Still, everyone knew it could easily fail. What if the intelligence the Allies had received about the Nazis was wrong? What if Hitler already knew the invasion was coming?

What then?

As the Allied generals pondered these and other questions, they knew that the actions they planned were dangerous, but they also knew *the greatest risk was doing nothing.*

This is something America learned the hard way. For several years England had been pleading with the United States to join the war effort. Even though we had watched Hitler and his army annihilate nation after nation, we stayed on the sidelines. After all, the war was on another continent, surely it would never hit our shores—or so we thought.

And then the Japanese bombed Pearl Harbor.

action saves lives

While it was sad that we had to wait until the enemy dealt us such a strong blow to get involved, the way the country responded once America entered the war was amazing. When the men went to combat, the women took their places in the factories to keep the nation well-supplied. People lived on rations and paid whatever price necessary to win the war. "Whatever it takes" was their rally cry.

a new war

Why talk about war? Because there are well-armed enemies marching across this land, leaving many young hearts and minds in their wake. I have seen the wounding effects and listened to the stories of many, many teens hurting, broken, and bleeding (some by their own hands). I have seen the signs of war, and so have you. Just look around you. Stop for a second and think about those around you in your school. How many of them are bound in depression, thinking about suicide, or cutting themselves? How many are escaping through drugs and alcohol? How many are destroying their purity with the opposite sex, or the same sex? The signs of war are everywhere, but too few seem to realize that the adversary is at our door.

the face of the enemy

Most of us had never heard the name "Al-Qaeda" before 9/11. But now the terrorist group and its leader, Osama Bin Laden, have become household names. We have since learned that this group was organized and well-funded. This newly revealed enemy is not a bunch of simple-minded people living in the desert with a few machine guns. They are smart, sophisticated, and well-trained.

Your spiritual enemies are no different.

They are deeply-funded and very organized. Just like Al-Qaeda, virtue-terrorists have a detailed plan for your life. They use their technology and marketing to create a culture of destruction, custom-made for your generation. For example, consider MTV, whose parent company is Viacom. While MTV would never say its chief aim is to "wipe out a generation," they are doing so by seeking to make money off of your mind and your body—no matter what it takes. Do you think they care? No way. Why should they?

They made $6.84 billion off of you and your friends in one year alone.[1]

They are effective at advancing their agenda. These enemies of morality have been so successful at advancing their agenda that tons of Christian young people have been duped. I see it all the time. They become numb and unaware of how the enemy is slithering into different areas of their life. They are hit from so many angles, that over time they see ungodliness as "normal." As a result, they let down their guard and start voluntarily soaking up the enemy's influence.

Pretty soon, you see them on the casualty list.

a call to action

It's time to wake up and realize there is a real war going on for your generation. Just like Hitler, your enemy is not playing games. He has something to gain by destroying your life. The Bible makes this very clear in John 10:10, "the thief comes only to steal and kill and destroy."

I began with the story of the Nazis in World War II because it is a great example of a dangerous enemy we tried to ignore but who wouldn't go away. My hope and prayer is that your generation will rise up together against a shrewd, relentless, and well-funded enemy.

I have pledged my life to help you do just that.

battle plan

As you read through this book, you'll see a battle plan unfold. You'll see ways to rise up with others from your generation and make a difference in this war. God is calling your name to the battle by giving you this book. *Your generation awaits your response.*

Here is a summary of how you can enter the battle:

❏ Go online at **www.battlecry.com** and enlist today in the BattleCry Coalition to receive regular e-mail updates on exactly how to pray and stay involved in practical ways of reaching out to your generation.

❏ Find some friends to go through this book with you. There's power in numbers: inspire others to get committed to your generation with you.

❏ Give a copy of *BattleCry for a Generation* to your pastor and youth pastor. Follow up with them once they have read it. Brainstorm together: What steps can you all take as a church to reach out to teens in your community?

❏ Talk to your local youth pastor/leader to find out how your gifts can be used to expand the youth ministry.

As you read this book, keep asking yourself: What is touching my heart right now? What need can I meet? What gift can I use? Remember: Real lives are waiting on the other side of your obedience. Stop right now and look over the above lists. Check which actions intrigue you even now. Everyone can do something. Come back to these lists frequently as you read each chapter.

For all the practical ideas mentioned in this book, there are a thousand more ways to enlist your energies in this cause. It will take all of us—that includes you.

Today is your D-Day.

CHAPTER ONE

the car's on fire

Chances are you didn't wake up this morning and think, "Today, I'll be a hero." Opportunities for acts of heroism rarely show up on our weekly list of things to do. Instead they seem to come when we least expect them, demanding split-second decisions that often demand great personal risk.

At least that's the way it happened for my brother Ralph.

One Sunday morning, Ralph steered his car out of a congested, post-service church parking lot. In the car ahead of him were two teenage girls. About a mile down the road, the girls halted their vehicle at a four-way stop, then proceeded carefully into the intersection. Ralph, his own car packed full with his wife and five small children, waited his turn to follow.

Without warning, a pickup truck sped through the intersection and slammed broadside into the car containing the two teenage girls. Ralph watched in disbelief as the driver, 17-year-old Ashley, was thrown from the car and killed instantly. Then his disbelief turned to horror as the car burst into flames, trapping the second girl, 14-year-old Amy, unconscious inside. Ralph was suddenly out of his car and racing toward the burning vehicle. Somehow he managed to pry open the car door and, grabbing the belt loops of the limp and helpless teenager, freed Amy from the burning car. Soon after Ralph pulled Amy to safety, paramedics whisked her away to the hospital where she recovered fully.

Suddenly Ralph was the town hero. He had saved a girl's life! Congratulations began pouring in from all over town, including the mayor's office. The local paper featured an article about Ralph's selfless act. When I discovered what had happened, I called Ralph to express my amazement at his courage. I tried to imagine what had inspired this father of five to risk everything—his personal safety, his family, his life—for a girl he barely knew.

Finally I asked him the question: "What were you thinking? I mean, what was going through your mind as you approached that burning car?"

"You know, Ron," Ralph replied, "I didn't do anything that anyone else in my position wouldn't have done. I don't know how I did it. All I know is that *when the car is on fire, you do whatever you have to do to get everybody out!*"

The situation facing your generation today is similar to what my brother encountered that Sunday morning. Things like suicide, abortion, alcohol, drug abuse, and violence are like fiery flames that are currently licking at the wreckage of many young lives. The car is on fire and this generation of youth in America, your generation, is trapped inside!

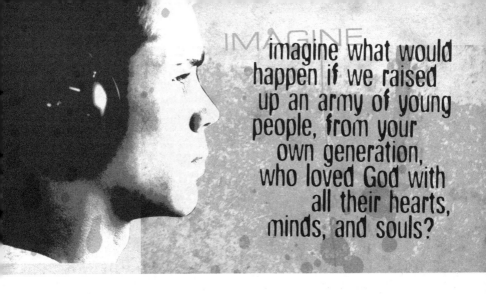

imagine what would happen if we raised up an army of young people, from your own generation, who loved God with all their hearts, minds, and souls?

nation at a crossroads

Have you ever thought about the fact that *you* are the future of this nation? Often times when we're young, we don't think about it much. We simply think that a bunch of "older" people are running the country and shaping our society. The truth is, in a few short years, that's going to be you. And out of all the generations that our country has ever seen, yours will have a greater influence in shaping the future of the United States than any other in world history.

Research tells us that your generation (referred to as the Bridgers or Millenials) is the largest American generation that ever existed. In fact, right now, there are 33 million teenagers in the United States.[2] So as your generation assumes more and more influence in our nation, it will do so with more force than any other generation before. Whichever direction your generation goes, it will pull the entire country with it. Needless to say you can see why it is so important that the hearts of your generation are captured for Christ.

Can you dream with me for a second and imagine what would happen if we raised up an army of young people, from your own generation, who loved God with all their hearts, minds, and souls?

Together we can take a stand and rescue this generation from the burning car.

What would that do for your future, my future, for the future of America? Can you imagine living in a nation where God is revered again? Can you picture living in an America where violent crime ceases to be a major problem, divorce becomes uncommon, drug and alcohol use fall to historic lows, and biblical values are taught to your future kids when they get into school?

Rather that moving toward that dream, though, it seems that the percentage of Bible-based believers has been steadily decreasing for a long time.

- *Builders (born 1927-1945): 65 percent Bible-based believers*
- *Boomers (born 1946-1964): 35 percent Bible-based believers*
- *Busters (born 1965-1983): 16 percent Bible-based believers*
- *Bridgers (or Millennials, born 1984 or later): 4 percent Bible-based believers*[3]

Think about what this means. Right now the Boomers are the most influential generation in our society. They hold most of the significant positions in government and business. With only 35 percent of them firmly believing in Scriptures, these have been the results in our culture:

- *Morally corrupt films and television programs*
- *An increasingly perverted music industry*
- *The pornographic invasion of the Internet*
- *Civil initiatives promoting gay marriage*
- *Battles to remove the Ten Commandments from public buildings, and fights to take "under God" out of our Pledge of Allegiance*

If these are the struggles we face now with 35 percent of the governing generation affirming a belief in Scripture, what will America be like when your generation assumes influence with only 4 percent currently claiming to be Bible-believing Christians? To put it another way: going from 35 percent to 4 percent would represent a 9-fold *decrease*. Can you imagine what would America be like if there were 9-times fewer committed Christians in our society?

Try to picture a society that mocks the fact that "under God" was *ever even in* our Pledge of Allegiance. Try to imagine the motto "In God we trust" taken off our money. Imagine all references to Christ and His cross removed from all emblems and city logos. Try to imagine a world where a pastor can go to jail for saying homosexuality is wrong.

Current news stories confirm that these unfortunate events are already happening here in the U.S. and in other nations around the world. If we think Christians are persecuted now in America, imagine being the laughingstock of society! Is this the future you want?

If nothing changes that is where America is headed.

For over 18 years, I've crisscrossed our country speaking to millions in your generation. I am compelled to do so because of how Jesus radically saved and changed me when I was a 16-year-old trapped in drug abuse and a broken home. Since then, He has given me the opportunity to share with millions of hurting teens how He alone has the power to heal shattered lives. I have seen the worst of the worst as I travel and conduct Acquire the Fire conferences weekend after weekend—and I know that no one is beyond the reach of God's loving hand. But never before have I felt so compelled to sound the alarm and to prepare you to take up arms in the battle of the new millennium.

A holy urgency burns in my soul that says NOW is the time we must work together to capture the hearts of everyone in your generation. It absolutely will not happen unless we enlist an army. We can make a difference, but it is going to take all of us. The time has long passed for teenagers to be reading this book and thinking, "Well I'm sure someone else will do something." We must all make a decision to be involved and find our God-given assignments as we read these pages.

We have a short 5-to-7 year window that will determine the fate of your generation and the future of our country. Research shows that once a person reaches 20-years-old, the odds of reaching that individual for Christ are nearly 10 to 1. That means that if they don't know Christ before they turn 20-years-old, there is only a 10% chance they will ever come to know Jesus. Research also tells us that right now 4.5 million teenagers turn 20-years-old each year and in the next 5 to 7 years the majority of your generation will already have passed through that window.[4] If we are going to make a difference now is the time we must act.

What we decide to do in the next 5 years will determine the next 50 to 100 years of American history.

Don't take these words of mine to just serve as another news flash or something that that makes you think, "Wow that sounds

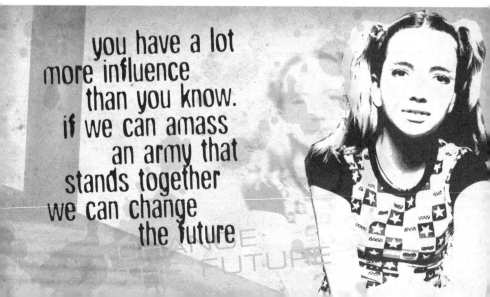

you have a lot more influence than you know. if we can amass an army that stands together we can change the future

just open your eyes and look around you, the car is on fire and your friends are inside

serious, I hope it works out." If we have that attitude, we will lose out and pay the price for our inactivity. You have a lot more influence than you know. If we can amass an army that stands together we can change the future.

This is not some pie in the sky pipe-dream. This is a radical call to an all-important generation. We've been backed up to the edge of the cliff and we cannot give any more ground. It's time for us to take a stand and fight back. While the enemy hates us with every fiber of his being, he is not so strong, nor the battle so large, for us to be defeated. We have the living God on our side. Think about it: "If God is for us, who can be against us?" (Rom. 8:31).

The Bible is full of examples of God using young people who were willing to take a stand and do incredible things for Him. When the rest of the army of Israel was cowering in fear of Goliath, God used a teenager named David to take the ugly guy out of the picture. When a Midianite army of 135,000 was coming against Israel, God used a teenager by the name of Gideon with only 300 of his peers to cause an entire army to cave in on itself. When God wanted to save the Israelites from genocide, He used a teenager named Esther to change the heart of the king and save His people from certain destruction. When Esther faced the crucial need of her people, she was asked to take a dangerous stand for her generation. Her Uncle Mordecai told her, "Who knows whether you have come to the kingdom for such a time as this?" (Esth. 4:14 NKJV).

I believe that it is the same for you, especially because you're reading this book. It did not fall in your hands by accident. Could it be that God has placed you on the earth for such a time as this to be a part of rescuing a generation—and possibly an entire nation?

Just open your eyes and look around you, The car is on fire and your friends are inside. Your brothers and sisters, your future husbands and wives, are all part of the generation caught in the burning car. This is who you are rescuing—not some abstract concept, but living, breathing souls.

The question is, what will you do? Will you just stand there and watch—or are you ready to join me and millions of your peers to rescue this generation? It's true that your name may not be in the local paper and the mayor may never commend your heroism, like what happened to my brother Ralph. But you can be sure that God will see your efforts and when we stand before Him, He will call you a hero.

Are you ready for a fight?

know your enemy

d-day

History tells us that if we're to win a war, then we must know our enemy well. The well-planned response to Hitler on D-Day is an example of this. This battle was successful because Eisenhower and his allies were able to predict the Führer's moves by studying his tactics and understanding the strengths and weaknesses of his army.

Sun–Zhu defines this philosophy in his classic war strategy manual called *The Art of War*, which has been read by successful military strategists for hundreds of years. He confirms the importance of reliable intelligence when he says, "If you know the enemy and know yourself, you need not fear the result of a hundred battles. If you know yourself but not the enemy, for every victory gained you will also suffer a defeat. If you know neither the enemy nor yourself, you will succumb in every battle."

The same philosophy that is used in natural wars is also true of spiritual wars. When Paul was addressing the church at Corinth in their own spiritual battle, he was able to give them specific instructions because he was "not unaware of his [the devil's] schemes" (2 Cor. 2:11).

who is the enemy?

Our enemy, the devil, is only able to exercise his power by invitation. That's why when he came to tempt Eve, he couldn't force her to eat the apple. Instead, he had to deceive her into taking that spiritually-fatal bite. His tactics are no different today. Satan is not able to *force* you to sin. If you're forced to do something, you cannot be held morally responsible. Instead, he goes to work on your mind, introducing tiny deceptions, one at a time. Then, little by little, when he has enough influence in your life, you begin following through on temptation. And just like Eve, each time we fall, our lives take a turn for the worse.

Maybe you are wondering how he brings about all this deception, creating such a stronghold in our minds that causes us to sin? He's successful because he's being invited to do it. Surprised? Over the next few chapters I will show you how the enemy has been using media to bring his acidic ideas right into our homes. The constant bombardment of unholy images from TV, the Internet, video

between movies and television, you will view an estimated 10,000 acts of violence each year

games, and movies, has provided him with more than enough means to dupe us a little at a time—until we're finally giving in to his agenda.

how bad is it?

If we are going to win the battle against your generation we had better start studying our enemy closely. Everyone knows, of course, there's a lot of bad stuff on television and on the Internet. But just how bad is it? Do you think you know? You may be surprised to find that you have become desensitized to what's out there—just because it's so common. Let's take a look at four of the most influencial forms of media in the world today.

Television and Movies: Have you noticed that so much of what is put in front of you on television and the movies is dripping with violence, sex, and alcohol? In fact nearly 61 percent of all television programming contains some sort of violence, with *children's* programming being the most brutal! Maybe you didn't realize how much of it was going in your mind, but between movies and television, you will view an estimated 10,000 acts of violence each year.[5]

And it's not just violence either. They are trying to brainwash you with sex too. The so-called "family hour" contains more than eight sexual incidents per hour. In fact, maybe you didn't know that if you are like most teens you will absorb over 15,000 sexual references this year.

If this isn't bad enough, on top of all the sex and violence, recent studies show that 70 percent of all prime-time programming depicted alcohol, tobacco, or illicit drug use.

And it doesn't stop there.

In addition to regular TV programming you are also subject to around 20,000 commercials each year, 2,000 of which will be push beer or wine. Doesn't it bother you to know that alcohol manufacturers spend $2 billion each year just to try to get you to drink? It bugs me to think that people would spend that much money to lure me into something that has ruined tens of thousands of lives—with no concern for me, as long as they make a buck.

If you are willingly exposing your mind to these pounding messages, you may find it helpful to know whose ideas you are listening to and watching. Sociologists conducted a survey of 104 of Hollywood's elite, asking the most influential writers and producers a number of ideological questions. The findings showed the following:

- *93 percent seldom or never go to worship services;*
- *97 percent believe in a woman's right to abort;*
- *5 percent strongly agree that homosexuality is wrong;*
- *16 percent agree that adultery is wrong;*
- *99 percent believe that television should be "more critical" of Judeo-Christian values.*[6]

Just think about this for a second. Would you choose to spend a few hours everyday listening to the thoughts, ideas, and beliefs of people who fit into the above categories? What if people with these beliefs kept coming to your house every day, asking if they could come in and persuade you about their values?

You would probably never let them through the door. You know if you stayed under the waterfall of their lies long enough, eventually it would affect you.

But if you think about it, that is exactly what's happening! Sure they use funny material and state-of-the-art technology, but they are still brainwashing you with ideas and beliefs that directly contradict what Jesus teaches us — and we are paying them to do it!

Music: The enemy isn't limited to television and movie screens. Most of today's hits are dishing up helpings of bile and vile, and pounding home the obscenities. Do you think I am going too far in saying that? Many of today's most popular artists such as Eminem, Nelly, and Kidd Rock have lyrics that could not even be published in this book.

So many young people say, "I don't listen to the words," but I have watched (at Acquire the Fire events) as we have brought out a music expert in the past. They interview kids about music all the time. For example, they would say a few words to a song and then ask who the artist was. Those same people who say they don't listen to the lyrics not only named the musician, but finished the verses!

There has been a fair amount of discussion over the last 50 years about what are called "subliminal messages" and their effect on our behaviors. One form of subliminal messages are little flashes of information that happen too quickly for our conscious mind to register. But they get buried deep in our subconscious minds. For example, one study showed that flashing a message such as "eat popcorn" as movie viewers awaited the start of the film increased popcorn sales by 58%. (This experiment was profiled in the book *The Hidden Persuaders* by Vance Packard.)

Even a split-second blip on a movie screen is able to affect our behavior. If this is true, than how long do you think you can continue keep putting music describing immoral sex and violence in your mind without it affecting your attitudes and behaviors?

Not long.

Video Games: In case you hadn't noticed, video games have come a long way from the hungry little Pac-Man. Today, video games are a $7 billion industry.[7] These 3-D animated extravaganzas have become a surreal world of raunch and gore that's intended to gut your imagination. In most cases, players are rewarded for acting out robberies, killings, and effective ways to solicit prostitutes. In "Sims 2," you even get to play God. The ad for its newest version boasts: "The Sims provide DNA data and inherited personality traits which let you control your computerized offspring from birth to death. Groom future generations, direct your own Sims movies, or simply enjoy the fruits of life without the burden of human interaction."

Even though the worst games are rated M (ironically, for "mature"), teens still play them. Some of the most popular games today center the entire object of the game around beating people up and killing them. For example, "Grand Theft Auto: San Andreas" is a popular game where players get to steal cars, kill people, and pick up prostitutes—and then go eat dinner!

The Internet: While the Internet has provided some great benefits to us, it has also become another area that the enemy has tried to monopolize in order to saturate your generation with ideas that will kill their spirits.

Many people go online to get e-mail, do some research, or chat with friends—and those things don't seem too bad at all. But

the devil is using media under the disguise of "fun" or "entertainment" to gain access to and pollute your minds

according to the study mentioned above, many people spend far more time online viewing "adult" web sites than they do the "safe" activities described above.[8]

Currently there are over 300,000 pornographic web sites for teens to explore on the Internet. You may think, *can't I just avoid these sites?* Unfortunately, it's not that easy. The National Center for Missing and Exploited Children found that 1 in 5 children ages 10-17, who regularly use the Internet, have received some sort of sexual solicitation online. 1 in 4 was *unwillingly* exposed to images of naked people or people having sex.[9]

The devil is using media under the disguise of "fun" or "entertainment" to gain access to and pollute your minds. The Bible says in 2 Corinthians 11:14, "Satan himself masquerades as an angel of light." If he were to show up as a drug pusher or a murderer, we would probably have no trouble turning away from him. So instead he uses things that are much harder to detect. Media has mass appeal in our society and is culturally acceptable. It is a normal part of our everyday lives. Everyone seems to have a TV, everyone goes to the movies, so we don't worry about it much or think about the effects it might be having on us. As a result, we become easy prey because we voluntarily let Lucifer into our minds.

The devil's duping reminds me of the battle of Troy. The famous legend tells the story of a battle raged against the city of Troy. Both sides fought valiantly, but they were getting nowhere after many years. So the Greek army designed a clever scheme to win the war. They built a huge hollow horse, as tall as a 5-story building, and left it on the shore—then appeared to be heading back home over the high seas.

When the Trojan army arrived, it looked like the Greek army had retreated and left the horse as a peace offering. So they rolled the large horse into their city and celebrated it as a symbol of their victory. What they did not know is that the horse was filled with enemy soldiers. In the middle of the night, the enemies emerged from the horse and opened the gates of the city to let the rest of the army in—and then they systematically destroyed the unsuspecting citizens.

The story of the Trojan horse reminds me so much of what is happening today. The enemy packages his deception in the form of cool-sounding music or fast-paced movies—and we buy into them. We fail to see the trap, so we take the enemy into our own minds. Just like the battle of Troy—once he is on the inside, he begins to reap havoc on our minds.

Often times we don't realize what's happened until it's too late.

what are the effects?

You may be thinking, *"Come on Ron, you are overreacting, does it really have that much of an effect on us?"* Often what we do is isolate one individual program, or video game, and dismiss its effects. But what we fail to understand is the cumulative effect of an invasive environment, an atmosphere that now overflows with sex and gore. Consider the power of this unending stream of perversity: it glazes, hazes, and raises you.

It glazes you. Have you ever been so fixed on the television screen that you were rude to a loved one who dared interrupt? You just didn't want to miss a single word! That what they call an "alpha state." Many teens, maybe even you, live in this type of media-induced trance day in and day out. Whether the source is movies, music, or the Internet, the addictive nature of the media can make our "real" lives and relationships fade into the background.

The trap is that for many it seems so much easier to remain frozen in an escapist glaze than to face real problems, real people, or real boredom. There are so many in your generation that have

the average teenager takes in over 18,000 hours of television by the time he or she graduates from high school

hard circumstances and tough situations in their lives that just will not go away. These challenges usually get worse when they are ignored. But the temptation to just escape into a fake world where you can be distracted from facing some of the difficulties of life sometimes seems too great. As a result of not facing life, we continue to deteriorate. We become like ostriches, who, when they see danger coming, stick their heads in the sand. They figure if they can't see it, it must have gone away!

Perhaps that's why more families own a television set than a telephone. The average teenager takes in over 18,000 hours of television by the time he or she graduates from high school—that's over 5,000 more hours than you will spend in your 12 years of classes! In fact, American children spend more time watching television than they spend on any other activity except sleeping.[10]

Your generation averages 16-to-17 hours per week watching television. If you add video games and movies, the average teenage image-consumer spends as many as 35-to-55 hours per week in front of a screen. With this level of media consumption, is it possible to think that you will be unaffected? In reality it is foolish to think that you can do anything for 35+ hours each week without it dramatically impacting your life.

It hazes you. After seeing and listening to so much bad stuff, here's what happens: *what's right and what's wrong* start to become a little hazy. In fact research says that 83% of your generation believes that truth is relative to the situation! According to this way of thinking, something can be true in one context, but not another. Your generation's idea of what is true and important has been shaped primarily by those who believe there are no absolutes.

Think about why so many in your generation wear tight, skimpy clothes that show way too much skin, or why profanity seems to be part of the normal vocabulary, or why so many now will argue that homosexuality really isn't wrong. You need to open your eyes. Do you think your friends at school all came to this conclusion on their own? Is it from their parents or the Bible? Or is it the constant and consistent influence of those who continue to convince you about what's cool and what to believe? Almost like a herd of cattle, so many just fall in line and allow themselves to be led into the fuzzy world of moral relativism.

It raises you. Research shows us we now have a generation that seems to reflect the values of the media more than it reflects the values of its parents. That is why research firms like Barna and Gallup find that it is hard to see much difference between the lifestyles of Christian and non-Christian teens.

While this may seem shocking to you, it shouldn't be. You have been trained to admire the same people that your non-Christian peers look up to. Christian and non-Christian teens cheer for the same pop musicians and movie stars— no matter what those stars say or do. As long as these celebrities remain famous, we are told that they are deemed worthy of honor. Not because of who they are, but simply because they are known by millions. This becomes a serious problem when we are asked to honor those who are undeserving just because they are celebrities. You see, when we exalt

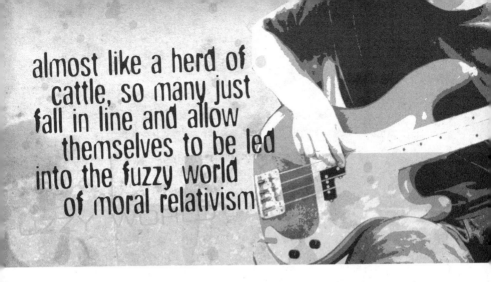

almost like a herd of cattle, so many just fall in line and allow themselves to be led into the fuzzy world of moral relativism

someone, we allow them to influence us and give them authority in our lives. People whom we truly admire . . .

> . . . *we listen to, not wanting to miss a single word;*
> . . . *we go out of our way to support and serve;*
> . . . *we emulate, because we want to be just like them.*

Think about it, when you find music you really like, don't you memorize the lyrics and read the musician's interviews? How many times have you or your friends gone out of your way to buy a concert ticket, even if it meant waiting up all night or even camping out? Or how many at your school do you see whose dress, and even mannerisms, are influenced by their favorite artists?

Ask yourself, if a person is involved in illegal drug use, criminal activity or even rape or adultery—but they happen to be famous—should we honor them? Absolutely not! But this is not what the media tells us. You could probably name 3 or 4 very famous people that do each of the things I mentioned above, and yet we are still told to hold them in high esteem by the media. Think about what this does to you over time. It consistently reinforces that character issues such as honor, integrity, and purity are

KNOW YOUR ENEMY

irrelevant. All that matters is social standing, popularity, and money.

What's even worse is that there are folks in the church who are giving honor to these immoral creeps. As a result, both Christians and non-Christians are allowing the same people to influence and shape them. No wonder so many Christian teens today look no different that those who do not profess to know Christ.

what does research say?

Countless studies prove what I've been saying. For example, it's clear that there's no gene for violence; it is a learned behavior. *Over 1,000 studies* including a report by the Surgeon General of the United States attest to more than a casual connection between media violence and aggressive behavior in some children. Such studies show that, the more lifelike the violence portrayed, the greater the likelihood it will be learned.[11] A study of 1,792 teens ages 12-17 showed that watching sex on television influences teens to have sex. Further studies have confirmed beyond a doubt that they are connected.[12]

I'm sure many of you remember one very obvious example of the connection between media violence and teen behavior on April 20, 1999. The 2 Colorado teens who killed 12 classmates at Columbine High School spent endless hours blasting make-believe opponents in violent video games, including the game "Doom."

- In November 2002, an Ohio girl was beaten to death by a 15-year-old boy with one of the posts from the victim's bed. (Investigators later discovered that the boy's favorite way to kill in the video game Grand Theft Auto was to use a baseball bat.) The boy then stole her car, as players do in the game. Witnesses say the murderer played the game for hours, turning into a "zombie" when he played.[13]

- In Michigan, during the Christmas season of 2003, witnesses say three "Grand Theft Auto 3" devotees played the game for hours, then hopped into their car and purposely ran over a man they didn't know (as players do in the game), went to breakfast, came back and stomped him into a coma (as players do in the game), and then went home and played the game some more.[14]

- On January 31, 2003, police in Oakland, California, arrested a group of young men, known as the "Nut Case" gang, for dozens of carjackings, robberies, and murders. Police say they were using "Grand Theft Auto 3" to train for these crimes and to get fired up to do them. Said one perpetrator: "We played the game by day and lived the game by night."[15]

- In Ft. Lauderdale, Florida, on February 10, 2002, 17-year-old Gorman Roberts was accused of pushing 5-year-old Jordan Payne into a canal and letting him drown. Roberts walked away laughing and told police later that he, Payne, and a third child had watched a World Wrestling Entertainment program featuring The Rock 3 days before the incident. Roberts' attorney, Ellis Rubin, said, "Little boys imitate what they see on television. If they hadn't been watching wrestling, none of this might have happened."[16]

- On July 1, 2001, 5 pupils at a school in Oldham, Manchester, England, turned up with flesh wounds on their forearms after copying a scene from an Eminem video in which a disturbed fan is seen slitting his wrists. The children, as young as 10-years-old, told teachers they had dismantled pencil sharpeners so they could use the blades to cut themselves.[17]

- A $246 million lawsuit was filed against the designer,

marketer, and a retailer of the video game series "Grand Theft Auto" by the families of 2 people shot by teenagers (in Knoxville, Tennessee) who were apparently inspired by the game. The suit claims that marketer Sony Computer Entertainment America, Inc., designers Take-Two Interactive Software and Rockstar Games, and Wal-Mart are liable for $46 million in compensatory damages and $200 million in punitive damages. Aaron Hamel, 45, a registered nurse, was killed. Kimberly Bede, 19, of Moneta, Virginia, was seriously wounded when their cars were hit on June 25 by .22-caliber bullets as they passed through the Great Smoky Mountains. Stepbrothers William Buckner, 16, and Joshua Buckner, 14, of Newport, were sentenced in August to an indefinite term in state custody after pleading guilty in juvenile court to reckless homicide, endangerment, and assault. The boys told investigators they got the rifles from a locked room in their home and decided to randomly shoot at tractor-trailer rigs, just like players do in the video game "Grand Theft Auto 3."[18]

After reading these you might be saying, "Well, Ron, aren't these extreme cases?" Yes, they are, but consider what all this buildup is doing to your mind. While most of these users may never make the headlines, their behaviors, thoughts, and lives were significantly altered by the constant bombardment of media influences.

For example, if someone poured acid on themselves to the

it is time for us to wake up and stop playing into the devil's hands by pretending everything's okay

point that it killed them, would it make any sense to say, "well I'm not that stupid, I'll just pour a little bit of acid on myself?" While it is true you may not die from it, pouring any amount of acid on yourself is not good for you and will have bad effects on your body. It is the same with these stories. Often we hear about them and write them off as extreme cases. While they may be extreme, why would we want to inject ourselves with the same things that drove them to that point? Just because we don't end up killing someone does not mean that it is not harming us. It's no wonder why the Scriptures warn us about this saying:

- Set your minds on the things above rather than earthly things (Col. 3:2);
- Love what is pure; hate what is evil; cling to what is good (Rom. 12:9);
- Avoid letting the world teach us to love what is evil or to envy the evil doer (Prov. 24:1);
- Stay away from the bins shoveling "beautiful garbage" (Ps. 101:3).

It is time for us to wake up and stop playing into the devil's hands by pretending everything's okay. And let's stop telling ourselves that we are not being affected despite all the research and real-life examples that prove otherwise. Consider the following quote by Joseph Stalin, a Russian dictator who was talking about the way to bring about the demise of a nation in one generation:

> *If we can effectively kill the national pride and patri-*
> *otism of just one generation, we have won that country.*
> *By making readily available drugs of various kinds, by*
> *giving a teenager alcohol, by praising his wildness, by*
> *strangling him with sex literature, and by advertising to*

*his and her psycho-political preparation, we create the
necessary attitude of chaos, idleness, and worthlessness.*

Open your eyes! This is exactly what the media is doing to
you. Only they are trying to tell you it won't hurt you—they're just
trying to get you to think it's cool. In reality it's a formula for
destruction. The only chance for winning over this garbage is for
your generation to realize that this is not just a bunch of extreme
moral talk, rather it is a real war, with real consequences, with real
casualties.

You must wake up and fight.

CHAPTER THREE

secondhand sex

You may not remember, but it was only a few short years ago when you could walk into almost any public place and have a powerful coughing fit. Cigarette smoke wafted from wall to wall in restaurants, office buildings, and hotel lobbies. If you weren't a smoker, you at least felt like one because you ended up breathing in the smoke from everyone around you who was *deliberately* sucking poison into their lungs.

But then people began to protest. They argued that smokers were violating fellow citizens' rights to breathe! Many of those who raised their voice were looked at as a small group of troublemakers trying to limit the rights of others. But the voice of those seeking "fresh air" became louder as more and more voiced their concerns.

Finally, scientists began studying the actual effects of "secondhand smoke." Once the harmful consequences became known, non-smokers had the ammunition they needed to battle for real change.

And they won.

As a result, laws were passed to forbid smoking in many public buildings. Huge, class-action lawsuits forced the producers of tobacco products to pay for the harm they'd done over the years. Bottom-line, no one should be allowed to profit while harming other people.

There exists today a very similar situation and it has to do with the "over-sexualization" of our society. You don't need to see any data to know that our society is now saturated with sensuality. It seems that everywhere you go someone is try to bombard you with sexual images. From magazines to billboards, to TV shows and commercials, to movies, to video games—you name it—it's everywhere. Even if you don't want to look at it, you can't help it. Just try to buy something at the grocery store without having sexual images forced on you by the magazines at the checkout stand. Like secondhand smoke, these images invade our public places and private spaces. Whether you like it or not you can't get away from it because it's all around you.

It's called secondhand sex.

the suffocation of secondhand sex

Secondhand sex is everywhere, and you are forced to breathe it in. There are virtually no safe zones, no protected public airwaves, no magazine racks that aren't blaring the latest "best sex tips" headline.

Even PG-rated movies that are supposed to be okay for children contain references to sex that would need explanation. Teen magazines try to sell you dangerous advice, like "how you'll know when it's time to have intercourse." In fact, to make you think that

secondhand sex is everywhere, and you are forced to breathe it in

sex is no big deal, these magazines don't even refer to it as intercourse anymore — it's just called "hooking up."

You might be saying, "Ron, I just don't think it's that big of a deal." People used to think the same thing when it came to secondhand smoke—until scientists proved otherwise. Researchers have begun to study secondhand sex as well. They've left no doubt about the harmful affects that this sensual bombardment is having on you.

A new study by the Medical Institute for Sexual Health found that the average teen spends 3 to 4 hours in front of the TV each day—which will include an average of 6.7 scenes with sexual topics every hour! On top of that the average teen listens to nearly 40 hours of radio each week and 42 percent of the top-selling CD's played on the radio contain sexual content that is either "pretty explicit" or "very explicit." Their research led Dr. Joe McIlhaney, Jr., one of the presidents in the industry to say, "kids are overexposed to sex." He also admits, "It's everywhere . . . even if they tried, kids can't escape it."[19]

I just gave you a few facts from TV and music, but imagine if you add all the influences from time spent online, watching movies, reading magazines, and the influence from peers. Does it have an effect? Researchers from the study concluded that teens constantly exposed to sexual content are "more likely that other adolescents" to have permissive attitudes toward premarital sex.

Not convinced that all this sexual brainwashing really affects you? A 2004 study by the RAND Corporation discovered:

SECONDHAND SEX

39

Teens who watch a lot of such sexualized program-ming are twice as likely to engage in sexual intercourse themselves. Rebecca Collins, the psychologist who led the study said, "This is the strongest evidence yet that the sexual content of television programs encourages adolescents to initiate sexual intercourse and other sexu-al activities. The impact of television viewing is so large that even a moderate shift in the sexual content of ado-lescent TV watching could have a substantial effect on their sexual behavior."[20]

Below are some other findings by the Alan Guttmacher Institute:

SEXUAL EXPOSURE OF TEENS

- Average age of first sex: 15.8 years
- Average length of first sexual relationship: 3.8 months
- 24.3% of adolescents reported having first sex during the same month as the start of the relationship (37.5% had sex 1 to 3 months after the start of the relationship and 40.1% after 4 months)
- 23.4% of first sexual relationships were "one-night stands" (21.2% for girls and 26.5% for guys)
- Girls reported their first sexual partner was 1.8 years older, on average; guys said 0.1 years younger
- 16.7% of adolescents (20.6% girls and 11.2% boys) who took virginity pledges became sexually active.[21]

It seems everyday I talk to the teens behind the statistics and hear the heartache and confusion they are going through trying to fight against the onslaught against them.

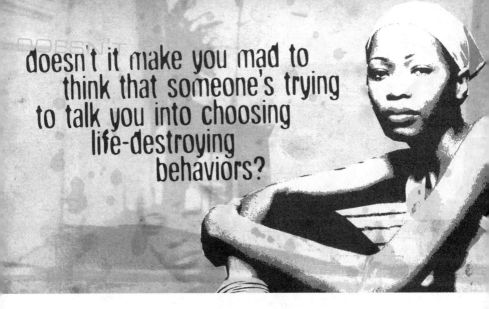

doesn't it make you mad to think that someone's trying to talk you into choosing life-destroying behaviors?

- "I know the Bible says you can't have sex before marriage. But why can't you, if you're in love with the person? It doesn't feel wrong." — Kendra, 14
- "My boyfriend and I don't want to mess around anymore. But how do we keep this commitment? I never realized how powerful passion can be." — Shari, 15
- "Kids at school are pressuring me and my girlfriend to have sex. I want to wait until marriage, but I worry about how this makes me look." — Darryl, 17
- "I feel cut off from God. I want to do what's right, but I can't seem to. Recently I had sex with a guy, thinking that it would bring us closer. I know now that was a mistake, and I feel totally ashamed."—Aimee, 16

Perhaps you can relate to these young people who have learned too much, too early, by their exposure to secondhand sex. Their minds have been violated, and they have lost the innocence and purity that God intended only for intimacy in marriage.

As we've seen, science has now proven the devastating,

destructive connection between this overexposure to sex and a person's behavior. So many from your generation have lost their virginity, their physical health, and their moral compass. Many have lost their dreams by getting pregnant out of wedlock—and a lot of them have lost their babies in this process.

Some have even lost their lives.

Doesn't it make you mad to think that someone's trying to talk you into choosing life-destroying behaviors? Think about your future husband or wife—right now the same thing is being done to him or her. And why? So people can make money.

I have heard people say that companies like MTV "care about teens" and "understand what teens are going through." They don't care about you! All they want is to take your money. They couldn't care less that what they are pushing may destroy your future and the future of your husband- or wife-to-be. They couldn't care less that you may have problems in your marriage because of the previous sexual experiences or thoughts that they have helped to initiate. They couldn't care less if you end up pregnant as a teen or with a STD. As they have proven, they will continue to exploit you in a harmful ways as long as they can get your money.

It would be bad enough if it stopped here. But I'm afraid that the world of the Internet is also full of sexual terrorists.

point-and-click porn

This great new technology we all benefit from can also be a portal for the pornography industry to lure you in. Just point and click to whatever you want—or don't want. It's almost impossible to avoid because you don't even have to go looking for it. By 1999 "one in five children between the ages of 10 and 17 received a sexual solicitation over the Internet."[22]

In fact, based on her Department of Justice study, Judith Reisman says that "much of the multi-billion dollar pornography industry focused on attracting 12 to 17-year-old boys to ensure life-time addict-consumers."[23] Is their plot to lure in young viewers like yourself working? It is obviously no coincidence that the largest consumers of Internet pornography are kids in the 12- to 17-age group.[24]

I hope you're beginning to see the trap that is being laid out for you. They give you a taste of lewd material from the store, and then from a commercial. You read more about it in a fashion maga-zine. Then you hear constant references to it in "family hour" sit-coms. Next you are bombarded with it by MTV. So when finally an e-mail comes that allows you to see a porn site, you have already been baited and are ripe to become addicted.

Is their strategy working?

Family Safe Media reports that 80 percent of 15- to 17-year-olds have had multiple hard-core porn exposures. And 90 percent of 8- to 16-year-olds have viewed porn online (most while doing homework).[25] That means that you and your future spouse have more than likely already been victims.

getting an extreme brain makeover

I want to show you some of the research that has been discov-ered about what pornography does to your brain. While some quotes may seem confusing at first, I want you to see the actual quotes to see that this is not just my opinion but medical fact.

In the 1970s, it was discovered that the viewing of pornogra-phy can actually permanently change your brain! Almost all teens have had exposure to sexual images and most are exposed on a repeated basis. Each time this happens, your mind is actually restructured through pornography's "erotoxins." Erotoxins is a type of brain poisoning. For more explanation check out what Dr. Judith Reisman says:

Thanks to the latest advances in neuroscience [the study of the brain], we now know that pornographic visual images imprint and alter the brain, triggering an instant, involuntary, but lasting, biochemical memory trail, arguably subverting the First Amendment by over-riding the cognitive speech process. This is true of so-called "soft-core" and "hard-core" pornography. And once new neuro-chemical pathways are established they are difficult or impossible to delete.

Pornographic images also cause secretion of the body's "fight or flight" sex hormones. This triggers exci-tatory transmitters and produces non-rational, involun-tary reactions; intense arousal states that overlap sexual lust—now with fear, shame, and/or hostility and violence. Media erotic fantasies become deeply imbedded, com-monly coarsening, confusing, motivating, and addicting many of those exposed. Pornography triggers myriad kinds of internal, natural drugs that mimic the "high" from a street drug. Addiction to pornography is addiction to what I call erotoxins—mind-altering drugs produced by the viewer's own brain.

How does this "brain sabotage" occur? Brain

Photo © Brand X Pictures

every single time
you view pornography,
it changes your brain in a
negative way and brings
you closer to addiction

scientists tell us that "in 3/10 of a second a visual image
passes from the eye through the brain, and whether or
not one wants to, the brain is structurally changed and
memories are created. We literally 'grow new brain' with
each visual experience."[26]

In case you didn't catch it, Dr. Reisman was saying that every single time you view pornography, whether it is "soft-core" or "hard-core," it changes your brain in a negative way and brings you closer to addiction. Pornography creates memory trails and feelings that are almost impossible to undo.

permanent damage

As the images of pornography continue to be imprinted on the brain, it is next to impossible to return your mind to its normal state. In fact, the U.S. Government Accounting Office showed no success rate for sex offender "treatment."[27] Why? Because according to Dr. Mary Anne Layden, "Images dominate rational thought, especially in the teenage developing brain."[28] What this means is that these images, and what they do to our brains, are so powerful that they override our ability to think rationally.

Dr. Reisman explains it further when she said the human brain obeys a "law of strength." That means, "strong, fearful, arousing, and confusing sexual and sado-sexual images will always dominate, occupy, and colonize the brain and displace cognition, despite any disclaimers used in "sex education."[29] She is saying that the brain obeys whatever is the strongest impulse at the time, the brain gives attention to that thought. As a result, any thoughts that are powerful or fearful or arousing will always win out for our brains' attention.

Even if our brains hold logical information about why we should not have sex, our brains will override those thoughts in the moment because the arousing pornographic thought is stronger and will win our brain's attention.

it's all about the gateway

You have probably heard of physical addictions to things like drugs and alcohol, but the concept of a mental addiction to something like pornography may be somewhat new. In reality both happen in much the same way. When talking about drug addiction, most hard-core drug addiction starts with what are called "gateway drugs." It is a proven fact that most kids who use illicit drugs started out with an addiction to alcohol or tobacco.[30]

Simply put, gateway drug use leads to hard-core drug use. The Child Trends Data Bank confirms this when it says "youth who are known to use one substance often use other substances as well."[31] Because of this gateway concept, the anti-drug movement strives to curb the access and usage of gateway drugs in order to keep serious addictions to a minimum.

The point is this: The "soft porn" of MTV, movies, and the music industry are serving as a gateway to harder-core pornography.

When you consider the size of the porn industry, it's clear that the gateway influences are doing their job. Just how big is the porn industry? It's about 57 billion dollars per year big. And just how big is that? Well it is bigger than the revenue grossed by all the teams in the National Football League, all the teams in the National Basketball Association, all the teams in the National Hockey League, and all the teams in Major League Baseball—combined! This industry is huge and it's getting bigger every day as they pull more and more of you into their clutches.

It is hard to deny that pornography (namely, any kind of sexually-explicit material or programming) may be the most prevalent and most destructive issue facing your generation.

In the chapter ahead we'll look at what these trends will mean to your generation.

CHAPTER FOUR

destruction of a generation

We know things are sliding downhill, but just how far have they gone? Just to give you an example, in 1940 teachers were asked to identify the top problems in public schools. They answered, "talking out of turn, chewing gum, making noise." In 1990 when teachers were asked the same questions their responses were, "drug and alcohol abuse, pregnancy, suicide, rape, robbery, and assault."[32]

This is a massive downward shift for just a 50-year period. How did it happen? Certain societal trends have gradually produced this generation-corrupting situation. Here are some of the trends over the last several decades that have led to the situations you are living in each day.

A business-dominated culture takes over. Numerous and simultaneous changes suggest that our world may, in fact, be catapulting toward a new era, undergoing a massive and foundational shift. Consider:

SEISMIC CULTURAL SHIFTS

- *From the time of Adam until the Israelites crossed over into the Promised Land, families and tribes ruled the world.*
- *From the time of Joshua until the crucifixion of Christ, armies ruled the world.*
- *From the time of Rome until the Age of Enlightenment, religion ruled the world.*
- *From the Age of Enlightenment until the fall of Communism, politics ruled the world.*
- *From the fall of the Berlin Wall for as far as the mind can imagine, business will rule the world.*

Maybe you haven't noticed but business now dominates our society. A predominant philosophy is *"If I have the ability to make money at something, then I have the right to do it."* So as long as I can do it, I should do it.

The problem with this worldview is that it takes all morality out of the decision. It doesn't matter if a particular product hurts people. It doesn't matter what the long term effects will be. As long as they can make a profit, it shouldn't matter.

Unfortunately, the approach is well-accepted by our society. Violent video games, for example, sell quite well. But as a result, many young minds today have been softened to the idea of beating and killing another human being. We have the recent story from

Houston of an 11-year-old killing his father, shooting him through the back seat of the family car. Because there are no parameters for what is acceptable sexual content in the media, we hear of another 11-year-old boy molesting an 87-year-old woman. Now you might be thinking, "ya, but those are extreme cases," and they are. But they are examples of the damage all these influences have caused to young minds and to our society as a whole. Just look at some of the everyday examples.

A morally bankrupt climate has arisen. You need to look no further than an average day at the mall to see how great our lack of morality is.

- You walk past the Victoria's Secret and glance into the storefront window: Your eyes fall upon massive posters of half-naked women. They are "dressed" and posed in ways that thoroughly mimic what used to only appear in pornographic magazines hidden behind counters just a short while ago. Now such scenes are on life-sized displays for all to see.
- You stroll into Abercrombie & Fitch to pick up a catalog: You end up paging through gay and lesbian pictures (set in strip clubs and shower rooms) that would have been unthinkable just a few years ago.

    The most overly gay-specific that Abercrombie has ever done, the images from the Winter 2000 issue of A&F Quarterly, the company's own magalouge, depict a double wedding of the Emerson family. Ironically, the reply card responses include: "Yes, I'd love to see two women get married." Predictably, the issue caused some controversy, something that A&F Quarterly has experienced before over depictions of nudity and the use of alcohol, due to the brand's popularity with youth . . .

After generations of invisibility, in these commercials guys actually get their guys, and gals get their gals. Kisses and affectionate displays are enjoyed by same-sex couples in the imagery. Transgendered persons are a non-issue, Gay Pride is celebrated, and some commercials even seem to sell the idea of being "gay" more than a product.[33]

At the very least this type of advertising is trying to teach you that to be valuable, you must flaunt your body. I don't know about you but I don't want these morally-void people shaping anyone's idea of how to dress, or telling people I care about what's acceptable.

A sex-saturated curriculum prevails. Formal sex education is standard practice is public schools. But perhaps you didn't know that the major sex education accreditation agencies are financially linked to big pornography companies (You can see Judith Reisman's book, *Kinsey, Crimes & Consequences* for full documentation of this fact). According to Judith Reisman, most

in the name of "free speech" and "business enterprise," your generation is paying a big price

accredited school sex educators deliver sexual information and images to children that are false and often pornographic. There are pure "abstinence educators," but none are officially accredited. This pornography as "education" can be very confusing and damaging to your minds because it comes with the school system's stamp of approval. After all usually we should be able to trust what is taught to us in classroom!

the price you pay

What do these societal trends end up costing you? They extract your purity, your innocence, and your perspective on marriage and intimacy. They rob you of the ability to have a healthy understanding of wholesome love, romance, and intimacy. In the name of "free speech" and "business enterprise," your generation is paying a big price.

Emotional Pain. Teenage sexual activity has generated wide-spread national concern. Looking at the numbers below it's no wonder:

- *Every day, 8,000 teenagers in the United States become infected by an STD.*
- *This year, nearly 3 million teens will become infected.*
- *About one-quarter of the nation's sexually-active teens have been infected by an STD.*
- *In 2000, some 240,000 children were born to girls age 18 or younger. Nearly all these teenage mothers were unmarried.*[34]

While you may have heard some of the above figures before, research has also found a less-publicized problem. When compared to teens who are not sexually active, teens who are active are significantly less likely to be happy, more likely to feel depressed, and more likely to attempt suicide.

It has been proven that so many who turn to sex are doing so more out of loneliness that out of lust. Chap Clark found in his study that sex, "is a temporary slave for the pain of loneliness resulting from abandonment."[35]

That is why the world's influence is so dangerous. All of us have a desire for love and affection, the question is what do we do with that longing? We know that God can meet the deepest needs in our lives and as we turn to Him, He can satisfy our hearts. But the problem for many in your generation is when they go searching there are so many influences telling that options like sex are the answer. The statistics above are proof of the destructive effects of these godless societal influences. What saddens me the most is that so many don't care what they are doing to your generation— as long as they can make a buck doing it.

Addictive Rewiring. Another price this generation is paying for the sexual saturation of our society is the plague of addiction. As we discussed in the previous chapter, pornographic erotoxins instantly reach the right side of our brain and trigger excitatory transmitters that bypass any forces of resistance the brain may offer. The human brain is then restructured, altered, and permanently changed by each pornographic image. Once glimpsed on a

when compared to teens who are not sexually active, teens who are active are significantly less likely to be happy, more likely to feel depressed, and more likely to attempt suicide

billboard, television, computer screen, or magazine cover—whether or not you want this to happen—erotoxic images invade and occupy the human brain, mind, and memory. The chart below explains the facts in a little more detail.

BASIC PSYCHOPHARMACOLOGICAL DATA

- *Pornographic images are neurochemically processed as real in the teenage brain.[36] Penetrating as "excitatory transmissions. . . in less than 1/1000 of a second,"[37] pornography's erotoxins shape the teenage brain on all three brain levels—*

  __Stage 1:__ The teenage brain is "alert and aware" of pornography as "reality."

  __Stage 2:__ The teenage brain "stores" pornography as "environmental information."

  __Stage 3:__ By "monitoring and correcting" teenage conduct, pornography injures the teenage user's health and well-being.

- *Erotoxic fantasies invade and commonly overcome reality. Males (and more and more females) unconsciously seek to bond with the women they autoerotically bonded with as juveniles on magazine pages or on computer screens.[38]*

Because the addictive rewiring of the brain is so strong, it is almost as if choice is denied to the victim. Neurologist Richard Restak confirms this:

> *Thanks to the latest advances in neuroscience, we now know that emotionally-arousing images imprint and*

*alter the brain, triggering an instant, involuntary, but last-
ing, biochemical memory trail. This applies to so-called
"soft-core" and "hard-core" pornography. . . . Once
neurochemical pathways are established they are
difficult or impossible to delete.*"[39]

It has also been proven that during intercourse a "bonding"
hormone called oxytocin is triggered. Oxytocin basically works to
attach the lovers more deeply to one another.[40] Since God
intended sexual intercourse for marriage, this "bonding" hormone
serves as something that creates a special bond that no other relationship has. Over the course of time as this bond continues to
grow it enhances the intimacy that a husband and wife will experience. But one's capacity for this special bonding is weakened by
having sex with multiple partners or by repeated self-stimulation to
pornographic images. This road leads to many intimacy problems,
including impotence.

Sexual Abuse. Sexual abuse is another common side effect
of pornography. Dr. Victor Cline was commissioned by the U.S.
Department of Justice to conduct a study on the effects of dial-a-
porn on children (mostly pre-teens or early teens) who had been
involved with pornography. Every single one became addicted!

*Without exception, the children (girls as well as
boys) became hooked on this sex by phone and kept
going back for more and still more. . . . One 12-year-old
boy. . . listened to dial-a-porn for nearly two hours. . . . A
few days later he sexually assaulted a four-year-old girl in
his mother's day care center. He had never been exposed
to pornography before. He had never acted out sexually
before and was not a behavior problem in the home.*[41]

Below are just a few of the studies documenting pornography's relation to sexual abuse:

- A 1987 study found that women who were battered, or subjected to sexual aggression or humiliation, had partners who viewed "significantly more pornography than" that of a "mature university population."[42]
- A 1995 meta-analysis found that violent pornography [did] reinforce aggressive behavior and negative attitudes toward women.[43]
- In a U.S. study of teenagers exposed to hard-core pornography, "Two-thirds of the males and 40 percent of the females reported wanting to try out some of the behaviors they had witnessed. And 31 percent of males and 18 percent of the females admitted doing some of the things sexually they had seen in the pornography within a few days after exposure."[44]
- A 1987 panel of clinicians and researchers concluded that "pornography's erototoxins stimulate attitudes and behavior that lead to gravely negative consequences for individuals and for society, and that these outcomes impair the mental, emotional, and physical health of children and adults."[45]
- A 1993 study found, "Exposure to sexually-stimulating materials may elicit aggressive behavior in youth who are predisposed to aggression. Sexually violent and degrading material elicits greater rates of aggression and may negatively affect male attitudes toward women."[46]
- A 1984 evaluation of the increase in rape rates in various countries bears close correlation to the liberalizing of restrictions on pornography.[47]
- Three separate studies demonstrate that exposure to

violent pornography [did] increase males' laboratory aggression toward women.[48]

Marital Dysfunction. Think about the impact all of these influences will have on your future marriage. If we have a 50 percent divorce rate with 35 percent of the adults having core biblical beliefs. What might the divorce rate look like with only 4 percent of your generation having strong biblical beliefs?

We noted earlier that up to 90 percent of your generation has seen pornography online, and 80 percent of them have seen hardcore porn. Those percentages would undoubtedly be even higher if you were to consider the pornography seen in movies, magazines, and TV. What will this do for your marriage and the marriage of your peers? What will your home lives look like? How much has this already affected your future mate? What kind of families will your grandchildren grow up in?

I ask myself these questions daily as I wonder how my daughter is going to find a man for a husband who doesn't have a porn movie endlessly looping in his mind, forcing him to compare his wife to some fantasy.

On top of all this, there is another common side effect of pornography. It's called heterophobia. This is simply a big word for having a conscious or unconscious fear, distrust, and disappointment in the opposite sex. That may sound bad in itself, but it gets worse. Heterophobia produces impotence.

Think about this, researchers found that after exposing college men to many presentations of non-violent or "soft" erotoxins over only a six-week period, these formally "normal" college males:

- Developed an increased callousness toward women, and would trivialize rape, while some rejected the idea that rape is a crime;

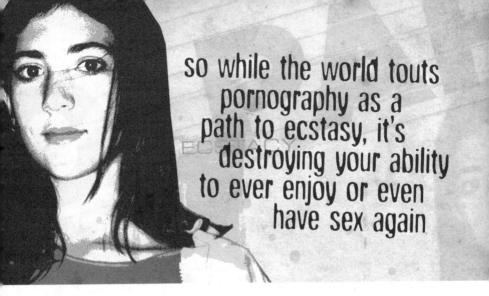

so while the world touts pornography as a path to ecstasy, it's destroying your ability to ever enjoy or even have sex again

- Needed more deviant, bizarre, or violent types of pornography because normal sex no longer excited;
- Devalued marriage, doubted it would last, viewed having multiple sex partners as normal and healthy behavior.[49]

Can the enemy's attack be any more clear? The temptation says don't restrict yourself, look at whatever you want, have sex as much as you can—hey it's a free country. Everyone is doing it. Or at least that's what the media tells you. So your young generation, ignorant of the dangers, jumps in head on. As a result, they become slaves to the erotoxins in their brain which turns them into addicts. As they become addicted, they become calloused toward the opposite sex and even sex itself, only to end up unable to have sex at all. So while the world touts pornography as a path to ecstasy, it's destroying your ability to ever enjoy or even have sex again.

what are the spiritual and moral implications?

I've heard it said before, as I'm sure you have too: Christian standards are simply a convenient means of judging people or acting "holier than thou." But without a moral foundation, many aspects of our society and our lives begin to crumble. Without any standards, we have what we see happening with your generation right now. They are largely a generation that will listen to any music, watch any video, or go to any Internet site. As a result, the quality of their lives is spiraling down the drain. And the so-called teen experts of MTV and Hollywood are right there to draw you in and push you off the cliff. And if your life gets ruined in the process, well, "hey you should have known better" (they say). As long as they are getting your money, they don't care.

You are probably getting mad at this point. I have often thought, *Don't I have the right to take my daughter to the mall without somebody's lingerie 'secret'—and crude vision of womanhood—being imprinted on her brain?* Shouldn't you have the right to grow up in a clean environment? If you are like me, you are probably frustrated knowing that people are purposely destroying your chances to have a successful marriage and to enjoy the intimacy that God wants for you. I am tired of listening to these people who try to act like they are the only ones who understand you and who are "on your side"—when in reality they are destroying your life and future just to make a buck off of you.

Enough is enough! It's time for us to take a stand. We must move from simply understanding the crisis, to putting together a battle plan.

The rest of this book is dedicated to doing just that.

enough is enough! it's time for us to take a stand. we must move from simply understanding the crisis, to putting together a battle plan

CHAPTER FIVE
a real war

The words "war" and "battle" are deadly-accurate metaphors for what is facing your generation. Some folks imagine the devil as a mean little guy in red spandex, running around trying to goad people to do naughty things. Even though we know he is real, we rarely think of him as a dangerous, crafty murderer who'll take any opportunity to take a piece of our soul. However, that is exactly how the Bible speaks of the devil—as a fully-conscious and treacherous enemy who hates you and wants you spiritually dead.

- Be careful! Watch out for attacks from the devil, your
  great enemy. He prowls around like a roaring lion, looking

for some victim to devour (1 Peter 5:8 NLT).

- The thief comes only to steal and kill and destroy (John 10:10).

These are not cute analogies. These and other Scriptures give us clear warnings about the intent of the enemy. But because so many of us fail to see the real war that's going on around us, we've become easy target practice. While all of us feel the effects of his attacks, many do not fight back because we're ignorant about where these attacks are ultimately coming from.

Think about how ineffective officers would be if their troops kept getting hit by bullets, but those leaders never noticed. Imagine, day-after-day troops continuing to get shot—and more and more of them dying from those wounds. But instead of fighting back, the officers think, *I can't imagine where this is coming from — maybe somebody's shooting a gun into the air. Surely no one could be this malicious and cold-hearted.* So they just kept allowing themselves and their subordinates to get hit rather than waking up to the fact that there's a real enemy who has their hearts and brains in the crosshairs.

This example may seem absurd, but it's the attitude of many today. Despite the destroyed lives we see all around us, we continue to think, "That's just the way things are" rather than realizing we are under a deliberate, focused attack.

While it is obvious from God's Word that the devil hates us, he is not stupid. He uses socially-acceptable, under-the-radar methods to push his destructive agenda. As a result, many have been

while it is obvious from God's Word that the devil hates us, he is not stupid

caught with their guard down and have been deceived into not seeing the danger.

You've probably heard about this experiment: If you put a frog in a pot of warm water and slowly turn up the heat, the frog will never jump out. The dumb thing becomes too relaxed to escape, and so it eventually dies. The frog is unaware that there is any danger—until it's too late.

The same happens with many teenagers today. The enemy is slowly destroying the hearts, minds, and lives of those in your generation—and many don't even see the danger. We must open our eyes. This is a deadly, spiritual war.

Jesus knew long ago that our fight against the enemy would be fierce. The Scriptures confirm that we are in a battle and we must take on the *mentality* of a warrior.

Praise be to the LORD my Rock, who trains my hands for war, my fingers for battle.   —Psalm 144:1

Fight the good fight of the faith. Take hold of the eternal life to which you were called when you made your good confession in the presence of many witnesses.
                                                        —1 Timothy 6:12

Endure hardship with us like a good soldier of Christ Jesus.   —2 Timothy 2:3

Put on the full armor of God so that you can take your stand against the devil's schemes.   —Ephesians 6:11

The weapons we fight with are not the weapons of the world. On the contrary, they have divine power to demolish strongholds.   —2 Corinthians 10:4

Jesus, Himself, told us to run to the battle when He said, "From the days of John the Baptist until now, the kingdom of heaven has been forcefully advancing, and forceful men lay hold of it" (Matt. 11:12).

Can you hear what the Lord is saying here? He explains in this passage that ever since He arrived on the scene, things have not been business as usual. The time had come when advancing the kingdom of God would be met with great resistance from the enemy—so you must be prepared to be forceful, even defiant in the face of a remorseless opponent. Advancing the kingdom takes a lot more than just going to church and singing "Kum-ba-yah." You must change your attitude. Stop playing patty-cake with the devil. No more letting him destroy precious lives. You cannot just sit by and hope that the devil will just give up and stop fighting against you.

It'll never happen.

This is war. Jesus invites us to get into the action. The "forceful" ones, the ones who are willing to fight against the enemy, will be able to grab the kingdom with both hands and never let go. Jesus is looking for us to join Him in the battle of the ages—to

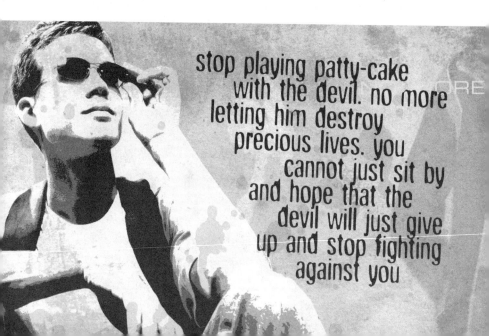

stop playing patty-cake with the devil. no more letting him destroy precious lives. you cannot just sit by and hope that the devil will just give up and stop fighting against you

aggressively jump into a fight that He started.

Think for a moment about all the Bible says about war, battle, and being a soldier. Now consider yourself and the other Christians around you.

Do they look like an army—or more like a social club?

There's a big difference:

CLEARLY CONTRASTING CALLINGS

A Club Member . . .	A Soldier . . .
▪ pursues a common interest.	▪ pursues a common mission.
▪ consumes some free time.	▪ dedicates a whole life.
▪ gathers acquaintances.	▪ gathers fellow warriors.
▪ passes the time to make the day fun.	▪ seizes the day to make the battle count.
▪ considers preparation as optional to staying involved.	▪ considers preparation as crucial to staying alive.
▪ finds courage unnecessary.	▪ finds courage indispensable.

did you join or enlist?

When you look at the differences between joining a club and enlisting in the army, which more closely describes your commitment level? Before you answer, think about it. So many young people today need to be enticed to come back to youth group each week and stay involved in the things of God. This isn't the attitude of a soldier. In an army, the commander doesn't beg soldiers to come back the next day or stay involved with what their unit is doing. They simply expect it because there is a high level of commitment because those soldiers took an oath. In God's army, the commander tells us: "Don't come back unless you are ready to lose it all."

In John chapter 6, some of Jesus' followers didn't like what Jesus was saying—so they stopped following Him. Then Jesus' disciples began to question Him too.

How do you think Jesus responded? Do you think He said, "I'm sorry, I don't want to offend anyone or make it too hard. Maybe I'll soften what I'm saying a bit, and make it easier for folks to swallow."

Nope.

Instead he turned to them and said, in essence, "anyone else want to leave?" (See John 6:66–67.)

Why would He act this way? Because Jesus Christ did not give His life to start a social club; His church was meant to be an army. He was trying to raise up disciples who would be able to stand strong when He passed the difficult job of advancing His kingdom to them.

In the army, screaming drill sergeants put soldiers through rigorous training because the officers know, in a short period of time, the future freedom and sovereignty of our nation will be in their hands. These commanders want to make sure their soldiers are trained and ready to stand in the face of the enemy, to obey orders even when they don't have the big picture, and to fight bravely and valiantly for a cause.

Jesus is trying to put that same heart in us. Jesus, too, is looking for people who will stand up in the face of the enemy, obey His Word even when they don't understand everything, and fight bravely for Him. Why? Because He trusts us with the advancement

Jesus Christ did not give His life to start a social club; His church was meant to be an army

of His kingdom and He knows the enemy will be there to push back at every turn. So we must be prepared with a steadfast, sold out commitment.

will you surrender the civilian life?

Army recruiters run offices all over America, looking for high school graduates on the verge of decision. These grads are thinking, *What am I going to do with my life?* You may have even seen them at your schools near graduation time. They get no bonus if young people just visit the office and talk about enlisting. It only counts when someone makes a decision and signs on the dotted line.

Too many Christians go to the "recruiter" on Sunday and Wednesday. They hear about the commitment of enlisting their lives for Christ's cause. They sing about the army and pray about joining. There may even be times where they experience great emotion, many tears, and a strong desire to finally commit and be a part of God's great cause. But, instead of making the life-altering decision of signing up, they come back again and again to the "recruiter's office."

But they never enlist.

Enlisting is much more than just showing up to the recruiter's office. It is a life-altering decision. From the moment you make that significant choice, your life is instantly changed. You commit your life to a cause. After that, your life belongs to someone else. You answer to the one to whom you have committed yourself, 24/7. You no longer have the final say-so over your life. The one with whom you have trusted everything has your life planned out for you from that moment on.

After enlisting in the military, you'd never say: "Hey, I know you had recommended doing some more push-ups and running today, but I think I'm going out to sit by the pool for a while." No.

You've given up the right to do what you want. You are in full submission to someone else.

Compare that level of commitment to your walk with Christ. Have you enlisted? Have you given up the ownership of your life to Him? Does your commitment better resemble the unwavering commitment of a soldier—or the casual commitment of a club member?

West Point is the United States Army's premier leadership training school. For 200 years this institution has been refining our military leadership to ensure that the U.S.A. has the finest army in the world. Visiting there, I wanted to observe the ceremony for all the freshmen "plebes" on their very first day. The families all gather on a grandstand with their soon-to-be freshmen. Before them lies a vast, manicured lawn leading to a huge stone structure with massive arches. Past those arches is West Point.

Those arches represent a point of no return.

After the commanders tell the plebes that they are "the nation's best," the plebes are asked to stand, walk down the steps

does your commitment better resemble the unwavering commitment of a soldier— or the casual commitment of a club member?

onto the lawn, and move toward the arches. As everyone else watches, without looking back, the plebes walk across the lawn away from civilian life and into their new life. If their parents or relatives stick around, they'll notice a complete transformation. Their hair is different, their clothes are different, their demeanor is different. West Point makes a dramatic statement about enlistment. To submit your life to a higher authority is a deliberate choice. You are pledging your life to a cause. It means turning your back on civilian life.

Too many of us as Christians have never walked away from civilian life. We continue to try to hold onto God and the world at the same time. Sure, we go to church and maybe even change our ways in a few areas. But the majority of our lives we keep to ourselves. We tell ourselves we are committed, but it's clear that we have never fully enlisted. Jesus clearly said to His disciples: "If anyone would come after me, he must deny himself and take up his cross and follow me. For whoever wants to save his life will lose it, but whoever loses his life for me will find it" (Matt. 16:24–25). This is His invitation to enlist, His call to deny ourselves, His challenge to make a radical and life-changing decision to find our assignment in His kingdom.

What's the difference between those who whole-heartedly follow Christ and those who are indistinguishable from the world? It's similar to the contrast between someone who is a big fan of the military verses a committed soldier.

The difference is the decision to enlist.

The apostle Paul confirms this when he said: "I have been crucified with Christ and I no longer live, but Christ lives in me" (Gal. 2:20). He also says that we've been "bought with a price" (1 Cor. 7:23). As soldiers we are no longer the owners of our lives. Our joy as a soldier is to gain our Commander's trust, accept His assignment for us, and throw our lives into accomplishing His mission for us.

Does all this sound extreme to you? Well you're right—it is—

but that is the point! Living for Christ was never meant to be a partway thing. It is a radical, life-changing decision to give the controls of your life over to God—forever. Think about that for a moment. Let that thought sink in. We use the word Christian so freely that it has been watered down. It's almost where if you're not a Muslim, Buddhist, or some other religion, then, by default, you are considered a Christian. Or you hear people say, "yeah, I believe in God, so I guess I'm a Christian"—yet their lives show no signs that they are followers of Christ.

May I remind you that Jesus never used the term Christian. When He called someone He said, "Follow me." His call was not to go to church or to simply claim that they had met Jesus or knew Him personally. Jesus called them to a radical commitment that resulted in a drastically changed life. That is why we use the example of enlisting in the army. Jesus was not looking for people to just mentally agree with Him. What He was, and still is looking for is dedicated followers.

Have you made a decision to turn over the controls of your life and acknowledge that He is Lord? That is what it means to enlist. That is what it means to be a Christ-follower. If we want to consider ourselves "Christians" or "followers of Christ" there is no other option. We must sign our lives over to Christ's control.

I hope you understand now that enlisting is not a docile decision. Enlisting in God's army requires a deep work in our hearts, an act of ultimate surrender.

Here's what I mean: One busy day I was called upon by the parents of a 17-year-old girl named Diana, who were visiting from out of town. These folks told me that Diana had been raised in church and was a good Christian. But then they told me this story: Diana had just returned from a mission trip with Teen Mania's Global Expeditions. Apparently as soon as Diana got off the plane, she called home. But instead of saying "Hi, I missed you," or telling

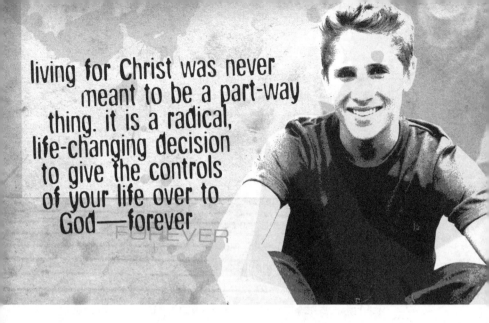

living for Christ was never meant to be a part-way thing. it is a radical, life-changing decision to give the controls of your life over to God—forever

her parents about the trip, she immediately demanded her mom to get something to write with.

> *"Mom, get a piece of paper and a pen!"*
>
> *"Hi, honey, how are you?"*
>
> *"Get a pen and paper right away!"*
>
> *"Why? What's the matter?"*
>
> *"Please just get a paper and pen right away!"*

After mom returned to the phone with the items, Diana said, "Write down this date." [The date she mentioned had occurred during the mission trip.]

> *"What is so important about this date, Diana?"*

Diana replied with a statement her parents had never heard before. Her mother looked at me with tears streaming down her cheeks as she told me Diana's words:

> *"Mom, that was the day that I died."*

Diana's mom then told me that her little girl has never been the same. Since returning home she has lived to serve, constantly reaching out to others in her school. She now exists to give her life away to reach others. Diana died to her selfish desires. She enlisted.

An enlisted soldier is not doing his commander a favor by tending to his assignment. He is doing his duty. He is doing what he signed up to do. If we are to change your generation and win this war, it is going to take enlisted soldiers—not charter club members. Our commitment can't be just a phase or some half-hearted effort. It is a moral obligation of every soldier to run to the fight and engage the enemy until the battle is won.

It is time to enlist. Are you ready?

I believe God has been anxiously awaiting the day that many of you would read these pages and make a decision once and for all to walk away from civilian life and sign the rights of your life away to the one who created you.

Before we continue with this book, if you are ready, will you join me in a prayer of enlistment into the army of our God?

My Father,

I ask you to forgive me for settling for mere club membership in Your family. I am desperately sorry for passively enjoying the goodness of Your forgiveness while others fight for souls. I ask You to take ownership of my will. I submit all my rights to You. I deny myself, refusing to live only for my own interests. I transfer the ownership of all that I am into Your hands. I will gladly live according to Your mandate. In response to Your love for me, I will learn to live outside my comfort zone so I can enter into the battle.

In Jesus' name I pray,
Amen.

CHAPTER SIX

a warrior sees the battle

Since God has clearly called us to be warriors, young men and women who have enlisted in His service, then we're going to have certain qualities that will apply to our service in the Kingdom.

A good warrior sees the battle and always keeps it at the forefront of his or her mind. As I've said, most Christians don't even realize there's a war going on. When they hear about the devil "fighting against us," they view it more as symbolic than a fierce struggle for their minds, hearts, and lives.

But look around you. There are people in your generation who are being taken out left and right. Open your eyes—it's not hard to see the masses of your generation falling into drugs, getting pregnant, losing their purity, and numbing their morals. How many people, just in your own school, do you know are hurting and broken and torn apart? I guarantee you, it's a painful war for them. Their wounds are deep.

This war is not being fought with tanks and bullets. The fight is a lot more subtle. Usually the devil is doing whatever he can to stay incognito. The war is being fought by small changes to our culture through media and other influences that end up taking our focus off of God. While it is true that this war is being fought by different means than most natural wars we are used to, the results are exactly the same: lives are destroyed.

mooks and midriffs

Did you know the MTV has a plan for your life? They want it to go in a particular direction. Their cradle-to-grave scheme is designed to capture your attention from the time you are young until you take your last breath. Maybe you were aware of their plan to turn America's youth into mooks and midriffs. Have your heard of them? Chuck Colson explains:

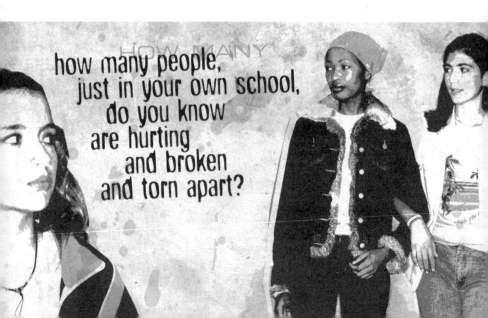

how many people, just in your own school, do you know are hurting and broken and torn apart?

*The mook is a character created to appeal to adoles-
cent males, characterized by "infantile, boorish behavior"
and trapped in a state of "perpetual adolescence." Mooks
are a staple on MTV.*

*The midriff is . . . a "highly sexualized, world-weary
sophisticate" who manages to retain a bit of the little
girl. Shows like Boston Public and singers like Britney
Spears provide America's midriffs-in-training with role
models to emulate."*[50]

Their goal is to keep teens from maturing so they continue to
be a prime audience for the kind of programming MTV offers. No
big deal you might say. Look around you. Mooks and midriffs
abound in our society. Just look at your school. How many Britney
Spears look-a-likes are there on your campus wearing short skirts
and half-shirts—acting out what they have come to believe is cool.

MTV's ideology has weaseled its way into our families. Your
generation has been called "the fatherless generation" because an
increasing number of men have fallen prey to the "mook"
mentality. They have not been equipped to grow up or handle
responsibility. As a result, we have situations where people marry
and have kids. But when the going gets tough, the dads take off,
leaving innocent kids in the wake of their irresponsibility. Many of
you may have personal experiences with situations such as these.
That's why each week in my travels, I see thousands stream forward asking God to help them forgive their mom and/or dad for the
tragic brokenness in which they've been raised. Their pain is
unbelievable. Their wounds range from the secrecy of emotional
abuse, to the desperate loneliness of Internet addiction, to the
misery of living under the same roof with parents who are complete
strangers to them.

the real effects of this war

Are you still skeptical this is a real war? Maybe you're thinking, *in a real war, people die.* OK. Well, in this war, people are dying too. Think about the number of abortions that happen each year. Or the fact that suicide is now the second-leading cause of death of adolescents.

Think about the struggle that has been taking place in Iraq for the last several years. That has been a real war. No one argues that. At the time this book was published, there had been close to 2,000 American casualties in that war.

Yet each year 750,000 people lose their lives in abortions from teenagers alone! That's not to mention other means, such as the drug and alcohol-related deaths. So while it may be harder to recognize right away, when you look at the results, this is as bloody as it gets. When is the last time a war has cost 750,000 American lives per year?

Maybe you would say, well Ron, *in real wars people get injured.* People are getting injured in this war too. Research tells us that 40 percent of your generation has inflicted some sort of self injury. 40 percent!

Well in a real war, *there is emotional trauma.* There is emotional trauma in this battle too. Just think about the massive emotional pain that comes from divorce, abuse, and unhealthy family situations. With all this information, you could argue that this may be the most devastating war that our nation has ever seen.

Take for example 13-year-old Beth. She is like so many that are hurting so much on the inside they decide to start cutting their bodies to distract themselves from the inner pain. She wrote me recently describing how she started:

> *Dear Ron, i'm in a really bad place right now. i'm just craving something, anything . . . i don't know what.*

i don't know what to do. i want my box cutter. i want to take a bunch of random pills again. i want to starve myself to death . . . idk. i haven't cut too bad for a while. i'm still eating, altho i hate myself for it. i haven't taken pills since the first/last time i did it a month ago. i just hate me . . . or maybe not. i just don't care about anything at all. it was so much easier not to care . . . but now i can't make myself care anymore . . . i don't know what to do. God feels sooo far away . . . i stopped even praying for a long time.

She then wrote this articulate poem:

I'm Fine

I bleed away my problems
I scratch them all away
My problems drip away from me
And slither down the drain
My problems are dissolved in crimson
My scarlet poison makes them die
A piece of metal shatters them
And through my veins the pieces fly
These scars upon my skin
Tell tales of secret pain
But come and listen to them
Of the truth I'm not ashamed
My problems are hidden from you

I hide them oh so well
What's wrong?
I tell you nothing
'Cause you can't save me from this hell

For Beth, this is a real war. She is shedding real blood.

we must have a wartime mentality

It's so crucial for us as warriors to realize how real this war is. Once that undeniable truth grabs us, it changes the way we think for the rest of our lives.

Maybe you have had a practice fire drill at your school before. During the drill everyone jokes around, no one really takes it seriously, while the teacher is fighting to get people to stop talking and follow directions.

But think how differently the scene would look if there were a real fire starting to engulf the school. The level of seriousness would change quite a bit, wouldn't it? People's eyes would be glued to the teacher, willing and ready to follow any directions she may give

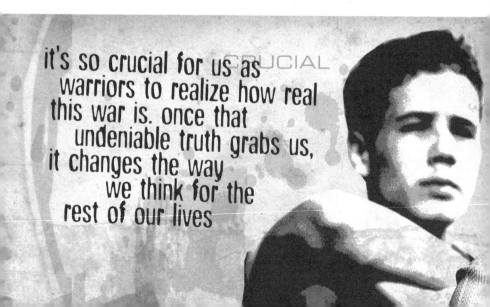

it's so crucial for us as warriors to realize how real this war is. once that undeniable truth grabs us, it changes the way we think for the rest of our lives

because they knew their lives and the lives of their friends were at stake.

Once we see this war for what it is, our attitude should change. We should go from a peacetime passivity to a wartime mentality. Consider some of the differences:

WARTIME VS PEACETIME MENTALITY

After the terrorist attacks on September 11, 2001, we Americans suddenly realized there is an enemy and that we must fight him. The president said, "We are now at war." But a war-time mentality is completely different from a peace-time mentality.

Peacetime Mentality

- Maintaining a self-improvement orientation: We seek the latest luxuries and newest toys will that will produce status.
- Focusing on personal economy: wages, promotions, career-planning—geared for advancement.

- Centering free time on recreational pursuits: supporting our entertainment needs.
- Complaining about the trivial: issues regarding routine inconveniences and discomfort.

- Imagining theoretical enemies.

Wartime Mentality

- Maintaining a survival orientation: We seek the absolute necessities and effective weapons that produce victory.
- Focusing on national economy: labor, production, and leadership —geared for winning.
- Giving free time to volunteer efforts: supporting our troops' needs.
- Enduring the "hardship as a soldier" (2 Tim. 2:3): issues regarding life-threatening trials and persecution.
- Facing real enemies.

Which one better characterizes your outlook?

As we move forward from this chapter, I want you to consider the words of John Eldredge in his book called *Waking the Dead*. He, too, was trying to get people to wake up to the war that is being waged by the enemy today.

> *"The world in which we live is a combat zone, a violent clash of kingdoms, a bitter struggle unto the death. I'm sorry if I'm the one to break this news to you: you were born into a world at war, and you will live all your days in the midst of a great battle, involving all the forces of heaven and hell and played out here on earth."* He goes on to say, *"Until we come to terms with war as the context of our days we will not understand life. We will misinterpret 90 percent of what is happening around us and to us."*

We must open our eyes. It is only when we see the battle for what it is that we will respond with the mentality of a warrior.

Will you pray this prayer with me?

Dear God, I thank You for opening my eyes to the battle that is going on all around me everyday. I pray that You would keep me from the deception of the enemy who would love keep me from rising up by deceiving me into thinking the war isn't real. God, I have enlisted with You, now open my eyes to see the battlefields in my life and in the life of my peers so I can join You in fighting against the enemy.

CHAPTER SEVEN

a warrior lives the code

When you join any branch of the military, you commit to certain obligations. Soldiers know that once they enlist, their lifestyles will change dramatically. They know the "code" before signing up, so it's no surprise when their commanding officer insists they get up at 4 A.M., exercise, do drills, and work hard. It's all part of the package. They have absolutely no say over their way of life any more. They knew that going into the deal.

It's not even an option for them to say to their commander, "I appreciate the fact that you want me to walk through that chin-deep cesspool carrying a rifle over my head—but I don't really feel like it." Even the thought of saying that is absurd. Without question, soldiers follow the established code for whichever branch of the military they are serving. They will obey every lawful order, without question or hesitation, even though doing so puts their lives on the line.

Joining God's army also requires lifestyle decisions that our Commander-in-Chief insists that we make. When we become Christians, we are declaring our loyalty to the person of Christ and to the way of life He requires of us. In Romans 6:17, Paul commends the Roman church on doing just that: "You wholeheartedly obeyed the form of teaching to which you were entrusted."

As enlisted warriors, we can't silently vote on which part of the Bible we feel like following, or treat God's commands as multiple-choice where we pick one and disregard the others. Yet so often, we say things like "I just don't feel led to do that" or "God hasn't convicted me of that area yet" or "well, my friends are doing it—and I need to maintain my outreach." But as warriors, we have forfeited the rights of our lives to Christ and must live the code He has outlined for His followers. It doesn't matter whether you feel led, convicted, or what your friends are doing. If it is in God's Word, we need to uphold His code.

Make the hard decisions before you *have* to make them. Picture someone pushing a beer toward you, holding up your hand, and saying "no." Decide now that you are not going to have *any* sexual contact (actual or virtual) with the opposite sex until you're married. [You won't believe how much pressure this will take off of you.] Decide *now* if following God is going to result in some sort of loss—the loss a friend, some degree of popularity, a false source of security—that you'll accept the pain of that loss and trust God to help you bear it.

Can you imagine what would happen in the military if you were to break the code, based on how you felt at the time? Imagine being confronted by a commanding officer and replying, "Well I just didn't feel led to follow that order," or "I didn't feel personally

when we become Christians, we are declaring our loyalty to the person of Christ and to the way of life He requires of us

convicted about that yet." I don't think you'd get away with that. Or what if you said, "Sir, don't get upset with me for disobeying your orders. Jack here did it, and I just followed his example. He's quite a celebrity, you know." Do you think the officer would say, "Oh, Jack did it too? Well in that case, don't worry about it. Can you get his autograph for me?"

Of course not! None of these attitudes would ever be tolerated in any branch of the military. But somehow, we have allowed ourselves to think it is okay to act like that in God's army.

I often hear people justify their continued disobedience to God's commands by saying, "Well, God knows my heart." This can be a very deceptive thought-process. While it is true that God does know our hearts, He also tells us that the truest reflection of what is in our hearts is our words and actions.

Matthew 12:35 says, "A good person produces good words from a good heart, and an evil person produces evil words from an evil heart" (NLT). What Jesus is saying here is that our words and resulting actions are simply an overflow of what resides deep within us. You may be a Christian and have many areas of your heart that are submitted to the Lord. However, looking for consistent,

habitual sin is often the best way to find areas of our hearts that are not yet submitted to God. Once we see these areas, we can either make excuses for them, or we acknowledge them for what they are and ask God to help us change.

Too often when we see areas of rebellion, instead of dealing decisively with them, we look at some of the good things in our lives and use them to "balance out" the sin in another area. If we continue to make excuses for our blatant disobedience, God's commands start getting fuzzy in our minds. We become slow to obey, and end up falling into some sort of deception. If we are going to be warriors for God, we need to stop hesitating and just obey God's orders.

I once heard a story of a guy who worked at a Christian college. On many occasions, he would caringly confront people whose lifestyle was violating God's Word. And there were others who had obvious gifts, and needed to use them because the need was great. Their assignment couldn't be clearer.

But he was often faced with the reply, "I just don't feel led." He became so tired of people using their feelings as an excuse for disobedience, that he bought a chunk of lead. When people would tell him they didn't feel led to do something God's Word was clearly instructing them to do, he'd ask them to rub the piece of lead. Then he'd say, "There now you have felt 'lead,' so go do it!"

As warriors, God is looking for the kind of commitment that says, "Even if I don't understand why you want me to do it, I will obey." But we tend to think, "Yes Lord, I will obey as long as it

if we are going to be warriors for God, we need to stop hesitating and just obey God's orders

makes sense, and I understand *why* you are asking me to do it." It's as if we think somehow that God is plotting to keep us from fun! So we doubt the intentions of the great Lover of our souls.

John 10:10 tells us that "The thief comes only to steal and kill and destroy; I have come that they may have life, and have it to the full." This verse tells us plainly that it is the devil who is trying to destroy our lives—and God who is trying to give us lives that are so full we can barely stand it. Strangely enough, we tend to get that verse backward. Somehow we get deceived into thinking God's commands are what's trying to take all our happiness away, and following the Enemy is where the fun's going to be.

I hear it all the time. So many young people are enticed with drinking and partying and all kinds of the things that the devil is selling them. When they hear how God commands us to live they think, "That's just a bunch of do's and don'ts," "The Bible is boring," or "The Bible is so restrictive, I want to be free."

This thinking proves that we are living in deception and it is not the attitude of an enlisted warrior. You may think the Bible sounds restrictive at times, especially when you compare it to what the world is trying to sell you.

But, I think you'd agree, there are certain situations where restrictions are good. Take a minefield, for example. If you were walking through a bomb-laden meadow, would you rather have a map with all the landmines marked, or would you rather say, "I don't need no stinking map; I want the freedom to run through this field unhindered by any restrictions"? I bet you'd choose the map.

Life in the war-zone is much the same. If we are not careful, there are many things that we can do in our lives that's like stepping onto a landmine. To put it delicately, if you step on one, the resulting explosion will inhibit your ability to walk through life—things like pregnancy, STDs, drug addictions, and others.

Because our loving God knows this, He tells us how to live. He tells us, "step here, don't step there." Then the devil comes along and says, "Nonsense, walk around wherever you want." So often we fall for his deception, step off God's path, and bounce up and down on a sinful landmine.

Now think about it for a second. Which sounds more restrictive to you: following the course God has outlined for us and getting to the other side safely, or stepping wherever you want, blowing off a leg and having to limp through the rest of your life? You see the devil's offers, which look freeing, but always lead to bondage. Christ gives us the crystal-clear guidelines to follow, which may initially look restrictive. But in the end they always lead to freedom. As warriors we need to see through the deception of the devil and decide to be wholeheartedly committed to following God's map. Bottomline, it's the only thing that brings the true happiness that most people think they'll find somewhere else.

When my daughter was small, if it looked like she was about to put a finger into an electrical socket, I would grab her hands and say a firm "No." If she reached again, I would swat her hand and say "No" even more firmly. If she persisted, I would pull her away and swat her bottom with a "No, no!"

In the mind of a toddler, this could seem harsh. I can picture her little mind thinking, *My Dad is so mean and nasty, why won't*

Photo © Big Cheese Photos

once you settle in your mind that God always has your best at heart, you will be able to obey Him—regardless of any losses you might have to endure.

he let me put my finger in those neat-looking holes in the wall?
What's the big deal? She probably thought I was keeping her from great fun. Being so young, she didn't understand the danger. As a loving father, I was only protecting her from being electrocuted and being unable to live a happy life—much less live at all.

It's the same with our Heavenly Father. He always knows what's best for us and He's always trying to protect us. As a result, we can obey the code He has laid out for us, even if we don't see the big picture. We can do this because whether He says "yes" or "no" we understand that He always has our best interests at heart. The devil has a significantly different set of interests in mind.

So many times this is where we go wrong. Somehow we get it into our heads that God is just preventing us from something we would enjoy. As long as you doubt God's sin-free intentions, you will have a hard time obeying Him. Once you settle in your mind that God always has your best at heart, you will be able to obey Him—regardless of any losses you might have to endure.

There are people who are hired to guard the President of the United States. Their commitment is to protect the President's life at all costs, even if it means giving their lives to keep him safe. In fact, if there is ever gunfire or a grenade, their job is to shield the President with their own bodies so they will be harmed instead of the President.

Now because the President knows their self-sacrificing mission, he'll do whatever they tell him—even though he's the most powerful man in the world. Imagine the President sitting down to his favorite barbeque dinner. Let's just say he hasn't eaten very much all day and he's very hungry. As he's about to take his first bite, one of the agents grabs him and says, "Mr. President, we believe this area is no longer safe and we have to leave right now."

Do you think the president would say, "Well I appreciate your recommendation, but this food looks so good, I'm going grab a few bites before we go." Of course not. Even if he didn't know what the specific danger was, he'd instantly get up, follow the ones committed to protecting him, and leave the pork chops behind. Why would the President walk away from something that seemed so desirable to him at the moment? Because he trusts his agents and knows they have his best interests in mind. Because he knows that they're willing to trade their lives for his safety, he follows them without hesitating.

Shouldn't we trust God this much?

We know from God's Word that He has already given His life for us. He was so committed to our spiritual safety, He was willing to die so that we wouldn't have to go to hell. Then He gave us His Word to follow so that we would be able to walk free from the enemy's bondage and live a life bursting with good things.

I can confidently tell you that God has great plans for your life. God never creates someone with a small destiny. But I can also tell you that the ones who will see these plans fully accomplished are the ones God will use to revolutionize the world.

God, I trust that You have my best interests at heart. Lord Jesus, because of Your willingness to die for me, I commit to live Your code. I ask you to help me obey what You have outlined for me in Your Word. Give me the strength to follow Your commands regardless of cost, convenience, or comfort. Help me obey You whether or not I feel like it—or understand why. Regardless of what the world tells me and what my friends do, I commit as a warrior in Your army, to follow Your Word, without hesitation.

In Jesus' name, Amen.

i can confidently tell you that God has great plans for your life

a soldier finds his assignment

I've never met anyone who enlisted in the army just so they could go to boot camp.

Soldiers know that boot camp is just preparatory; it's not the final goal. After this intense period of training, they expect to being assigned to a mission somewhere where they can make a difference. They know there's a place for them to plug in. When they've found that place, they know they'll be uniquely prepared to advance the cause of the army. This is the whole reason soldiers sign on the dotted line. They don't enlist in order to sit on the sidelines and watch the action from afar. They don't intend to just listen to the generals tell stories about great battles and glorious victories.

No, committed soldiers enlist because they want to, one day, tell their own stories.

enlist

A lot of Christians are just curious about the war. They're waiting around to see the highlights or hear reports from folks on the front line. They're completely unaware of their own mission. This is the proof that they haven't enlisted. Every soldier knows he or she has a place in the fight, an important task that must be done. Club members find jobs, hobbies, activities, and stuff to fill their time, but warriors understand they're on a specific assignment they have been given—and they are fully engaged in accomplishing that mission.

There is a special assignment in our warring kingdom, selected for you by God before the world even began. God custom-made every piece of you to be able to fill that gap and accomplish the assignment successfully. It's time for you to enlist! Your gifts and talents, your desires and interests, *everything* about you was designed to fill the role that God has assigned to you.

God told Jeremiah, "Before I formed you in the womb I knew you, before you were born I set you apart; I appointed you as a prophet to the nations" (Jer 1:5). Think about it. Long before you were born God set you apart for a specific role in His army. He hand-crafted everything about you and shaped you perfectly with the unique gifts and talents that would be necessary to accomplish your mission. One of the greatest joys in life is finding God's

Photo © Big Cheese Photos

don't ever think
that you can't
make a difference
in somebody's life

in a war zone, any person can save the life of another on any given day

assignment for you, the purpose for which you were custom-made. What is it that God set you apart in your mother's womb to accomplish? Do you know yet? Have you taken the time to seek God for your personal assignment in His army?

It's amazing to watch how God causes our assignments to intertwine with each other and to see how our lives are so dependent upon and affected by each other. Just think about how your life would be different if one or two significant people hadn't played their God-given role in your situation. Well, right now there are people on this earth that are waiting to be changed and rescued by you. Don't ever think you can't make a difference in somebody's life.

In the kingdom of God, the opportunities are endless.

So many times the devil deceives people into thinking their lives are not important. They think the outcome will be the same, whether or not they engage. But this is not true. Believing this is a trap of the enemy. He is terrified about what will happen when you find your assignment and plug in.

Have you ever seen soldiers being interviewed in a hospital bed after they've been seriously injured in a battle? Nine times out of 10, it seems that all they can think about it getting back with their buddies, and back out onto the battlefield. They understand the significance that a single person can make, especially when the fighting is fierce.

In a war zone, any person can save the life of another on any given day.

That's why the apostle Paul cried out, "Woe to me if I do not preach the gospel!" (1 Cor. 9:16). He knew that it was absolutely crucial that he discovered and completed his assignment. The same is true of us! Can you imagine what our lives would have been like if Paul had not found God's purpose for him? We would only have half the New Testament! You, too, have a great assignment from God. Other people's lives will be eternally affected and changed as you find your place in this battle.

Sadly, how many church-goers (do you think) assume that they've met their obligations to the Commander simply by showing up to services once or twice a week? They may watch in amazement when a few daring peers venture out to share their faith or travel to the mission field. They don't think or live like a warrior at all.

When I see this it makes me wonder, have they ever really enlisted?

It's like sitting at a ball game to root for our favorite team. We cheer for the pastor or youth pastor when they win a new Christian. We celebrate when a missionary tells of the souls they reached. We even congratulate a new believer when he comes to church for the first time. All this is normal for someone who isn't on the team, who's just sits in the stands. Think about it, when you go to a football game you cheer for the people who are playing and celebrate when they do well. But the key difference between a fan and a player is that the fans aren't actually out on the field. Once you are on the team, however, watching is no longer good enough. Sitting on the bench becomes excruciating. You want to play.

Warriors cry out to know their assignment. "Put me in, coach; I want to play!" Christians who've enlisted for spiritual battle come before God with humble hearts pleading, "Oh, Lord, show me my part; I want to be deployed into the battle for this generation. Please show me my mission!"

For the rest of the chapter I want to do just that. For too long we have sat on the sidelines as the enemy has just rolled over your generation with little resistance.

you are part of a massive army all across this nation that is fighting right along with you.

But the time has come for us to get off the sidelines and get into the game; to graduate from boot camp and run to the battle. The battle plan you're about to read can deal a mighty blow to our enemy over the next year. As you read these simple assignments, you need to know that there will be thousands of other teenagers doing the same thing. Know that as you respond to your orders, you are not alone. You are a part of a massive army all across this nation that is fighting right along with you. Together we're going to make a difference.

Multiply—win and disciple 7 people for Christ this year

The power of God is the only thing that can make a difference in this battle for your generation. If we are going to rescue your generation, we must introduce them to the only one who can save them: Jesus Christ. But we don't want to stop there. Too often we have settled for someone saying a prayer at an emotional moment in their lives and then have left them alone only to find their own way. In no time we find them right back where they started because there was no one to disciple them. We must commit not only to introduce them to Christ, but to disciple them and help them find their assignment in the battle.

One of the biggest problems in the body of Christ today is that we focus on adding to our Christian ranks rather than multiplying. If you look throughout Asia and South America, you'll find churches with 100,000 to 200,000 people! A church in Bogota, Columbia has 40,000 teens in their youth group—40,000! And many of their 13,000 cell groups are led by teenagers who are 14-, 15-, or 16-years old. They're taught while they're young to multiply their faith through first leading others to Christ and then discipling them. Soon those who have been discipled are bringing others to Christ and discipling them. Let's follow their lead and be so passionately in love with Jesus that we're contagious. We can't help but spread it! This isn't just an option. If we're going to take this generation, everybody reading this book needs to be a multiplier.

Maybe you are thinking, "I have never won anyone to the Lord—how do I do that?" Well there are lots of great tips out there for sharing Christ with others, but the good news is it's not that hard! It may seem scary at first, but in reality it is very simple.

Here are a few ideas that will help you be a vessel that God can use to bring people to Himself.

Look like Jesus. Jesus was a magnet for sinners. They seemed to seek Him out everywhere He went and wanted to be around Him. Sometimes I wonder if we have a hard time leading people to Christ because we need to look more like Jesus. This is a great place to start as you begin to work on drawing other people to God

Take inventory. Can people look at your life and know that you

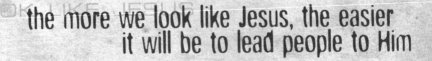

the more we look like Jesus, the easier it will be to lead people to Him

are a follower of Christ, that there is something different about you? Many times when we try to hard to fit in, we make our lives look as much like the world as possible. If this is happening, people are not going to see that we have a different hope and life on the inside of us, especially if we look like everyone else.

Ask yourself, are you listening to the same music, using the same language, and enjoying the same entertainment as your non-Christian friends? Do they have any reason, besides the fact that maybe you have told them, to know that you are a genuine Christian? If you could not speak, would your life to stand out like a light in the darkness? The best place to start is to find ways to get "yes" answers to these questions.

Sometimes kids think *if I am going to take a stand for Jesus, I have to be weird.* That's not true either. You don't have to have 50 Christian buttons on your backpack. You don't have to show up at school barefoot yelling "Jesus loves you!" in order to stand out for Christ.

But sometimes to avoid that extreme image we go too far the other way and think we are doing God a favor by looking like the rest of the world. This is not true either. Rather we are called to live lives that are *obviously* focused on the Lord. Our faith should be strong enough so that, while our friends are riding an emotional rollercoaster of sin, they can observe our stability. They'll see that our security comes from standing on the solid rock of faith. Even though they may not respond right away, they will reach for the most stable thing they know when things start to unravel. If you have continued to be a godly example to them, you'll be the one they come to. And that will be a great opportunity to lead them to Christ.

Another mistake is to think that looking like Jesus is mostly about what we *don't* do. As long as we don't get high and don't cuss and don't watch R-rated movies, then we have achieved some sort of a righteous standard that's supposed to make us stand out.

Even worse we often feel this gives us the right to condemn everyone else, even other Christians!

While it is true not doing those things are an important part of looking like Jesus, *what we do* is just as important as what we avoid. For example, Jesus commands us to love one another and to do to others and we would have them do to us. Think about what a difference that would make if you started to reach out and show others genuine love. You know who the outcasts are at your school. Go up to one this week, and just introduce yourself. What would happen if you began finding small ways like this to serve those around you at school? You know, start treating them the way you like to be treated. What if you really begin to live it out? If you are thirsty and want a pop, think, "I'm going to get one for somebody else too." Or "I like it when people sincerely compliment me, so I am going to start encouraging other people this way." "I like it when people keep their eyes glued to mine when I'm talking to them, so I am going to listen that attentively to others." "I really appreciate it when people do nice things for me out of the blue, so I am going to start providing some nice, unexpected surprises for others." Start living some of these things out, and pretty soon, people are going to start wondering what is positively different about you.

The more we look like Jesus, the easier it will be to lead people to Him.

Talk about Jesus. We're never going to lead people to Christ if we never talk about Him. There are dozens of ways to do this. You can simply bring God into your conversations by telling people about something that happened at your youth group or something that God has done in your life. For example: "I'm sorry, I can't make it on Saturday, my youth group is doing an outreach;" "Listen, I never swear that I'm going to do something; Jesus said let your yes be yes, and your no be no." "Hey, I'm going on a mission trip to

Uganda this summer; can I bring you back something?" Throw some "carrots" out there, and see if anyone comes back asking about all this faith stuff.

Ask people about themselves, and be genuinely interested in who they are as people. Eventually, some of these people are going to have the same interest in you. As you are getting to know people and they ask about what's important to you, share your testimony with them so they can know what God has done in your life. This is one of the most powerful ways to open a door about what God can do in their lives. You don't need to force God into every conversation. If you simply look for ways to talk about Jesus, you will find all kinds of opportunities in almost any discussion.

Some people have used much bolder approaches such as doing a short survey and having the last question be, "What do you think about God?" Their response serves as the lead into the conversation about faith. There are many ways to talk about Jesus. But when your goal is to come back and talk about how God really changed your life, it's never really a struggle to talk about it.

When you get a brand new CD that you love, or you hear of a great shirt sale going on somewhere, do you have a problem telling others? No, in fact you are excited to tell them about it *because you know what you have found would benefit them*. It's the same with Christ. Now you may be thinking, *What if they say no, or don't seem receptive?* Well if you are telling someone about the CD or sale I mentioned earlier, would you have an anxious fear over whether or not they will actually get the CD or go to the store you told them about? No, that's up to them. You simply want to tell them about it so they can take advantage of it—if they want to and when they're ready. In fact if they didn't respond positively, you would might think, *Hey, it's their loss.* Why is telling people about God any different? He's the greatest thing that's ever happened to us and just like anything good in our lives we shouldn't be hesitant to tell others—without worrying about how they're going to respond.

Prayer. Prayer is a huge part of seeing people come to Christ. Ephesians 6:12 tells us, "For our struggle is not against flesh and blood, but against the rulers, against the authorities, against the powers of this dark world and against the spiritual forces of evil in the heavenly realms."

As we have talked about all along, there is a real, spiritual battle going on for each of our lives. It's only through prayer that we break down the enemy's defenses. I would encourage you to pray for God's help everyday in talking to people about Christ. I know many teenagers who have put together a top-ten list of people they want to see saved. And then they pray for people on their list everyday—in addition to looking for opportunities to be a witness for Christ to them.

2 Corinthians 4:4 says, "Satan, the god of this evil world, has blinded the minds of those who don't believe, so they are unable to see the glorious light of the Good News that is shining upon them" (NLT). When the enemy is blinding someone, even when the Good News is right in front of them, they just can't see it. It is through prayer that this spiritual blindness is shattered so that their eyes can be opened.

Prayer makes everything we do more effective.

prayer makes everything we do more effective

Go on missions. Going on a mission trip is one of the greatest ways to bring people to Christ. Maybe you thought that missions was only for people who were overly-committed believers. But again, I hope this book is changing your mentality on what is supposed to be "normal" for the Christian. Missions is not for extreme Christians, it's for anyone who's enlisted.

Do you know what Jesus' final words on this earth to His disciples were? Jesus is getting ready to ascend into heaven. He is standing with His disciples, face-to-face, for the last time (at least until they'd see Him in heaven). Jesus has spent the last three years preparing these guys and teaching them many things. This was His final chance to impart one last piece of information, to remind them of the most important thing before He ascends.

Do you know what he told them?

In Matthew 28:19 Jesus said, "Therefore go and make disciples of all nations, baptizing them in the name of the Father and of the Son and of the Holy Spirit." Think about that. Jesus' last words, His final reminder to us, His disciples, essentially was this: "I have made a way for people to be free from sin and death. Now you take this message to the world." God actually commands all believers to go on missions! Are you a follower of Jesus? Then that means you! Start packing your bags.

I want to encourage you to pray about going on a mission trip this summer. I don't mean praying like, "God do You really want me to go?" I mean praying like, "God I know You've already called me to go, so I'm heading in that direction unless You stop me." Sometimes we see something in God's Word and then think we need to pray about whether or not it applies to us. Stop right there. If it's in God's Word, it applies to you as His follower.

For 18 years I have gone around the world on a missions trip every summer because God commands us to go. Again, there's nothing extreme about this. I am just following the orders that my

Commander-in-Chief has given me. This should be seen as ordinary behavior for followers of Christ.

I have also had the opportunity to help thousands of young people just like you go overseas each year through Global Expeditions. Every summer I see countless people around the world won to Christ by teenagers who are finally learning what it means to be a follower of Christ and obey His call to the mission field. Every summer people just like you are changing the world and reaching people for Christ.

Have you gone yet? If you haven't gone, or haven't for a long time, it's time to go. You are a follower of Christ now and that means obeying His command to reach the people of the earth.

Watch how God will change you as you step out in obedience to His Word. In fact, I would like to personally invite you to go on a mission trip with Global Expeditions. You can go online at **www.globalexpeditions.com** to check out the different trips that are available. You can also go with your church or youth group, but go! If there is no way you can go this summer, go as soon as you can. In the meantime, find some other people who are going and then support them in any way you can. As the warriors of our God that will defeat the kingdom of the enemy, we must be committed to reaching our own generation on our own turf—as well as reaching the nations for Christ.

double the size of your youth group

Now you might be saying "that isn't normal, Ron—my youth group hasn't grown that much in several years." Well you're right—this is extreme, but it can be done and it must be done. Think about it: if I offered you and every one in your youth group a billion dollars to double your youth group in one year (but you couldn't tell others about the bet), do you think you could do it? Sure you would. You'd find a way to do it no matter what it took. So if you know it's

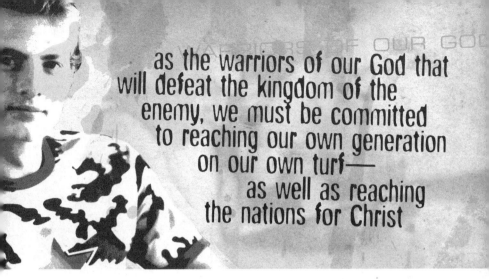

as the warriors of our God that will defeat the kingdom of the enemy, we must be committed to reaching our own generation on our own turf— as well as reaching the nations for Christ

possible and you'd do it for a billion dollars . . . shouldn't we be willing to do it for tens, hundreds, maybe even thousands of lives?

The honest truth is this, either tens of thousands of youth groups are going to double and triple, or we are going to lose a generation and a nation. So really there is not much choice. The time has come to throw away the old doubtful thinking and realize it can be done. We just need to do it.

Talk to your youth pastor and youth group. One of the first steps you can take is to talk to your youth pastor. You can share with him what God has put on your heart, and encourage him to get the book, *Battlecry for a Generation*. It is a book just like this one that I wrote for adults. Encourage that leader to get it and read it this week, because there is no time to waste. Then tell him your desire to see the youth group double in one year. Let him (or her) know that you are willing to do whatever it takes to see it happen.

After talking with your youth pastor, talk to your peers in the youth group. Encourage them to get a copy of this book and go through it with them. If they can't get it, share the one in your hands. Pass it around if necessary. You can use it as a tool to get them fired up and on board to do whatever it takes to see the youth group double.

Don't worry about the fact that some may not respond. Many of them will come around later and some may never at all. Don't spend your time worrying about those who haven't caught the vision yet—you're looking for those who will. Even if you only have a few who will fight this battle with you, it will help. If you have no one who seems ready to battle with you, that's okay too, God will sustain you. Just start moving forward and pray that God will bring others to fight along side you.

Make a plan. Your youth group will not double by itself. Even your excitement and passion will not alone cause your youth group to double. There needs to be some deliberate planning and commitment if you want to see results.

For example, I have heard of people who have started competitions in their youth groups where people have gotten points for bringing people to youth group and helping them get discipled. Then after a set period of time, whoever has the most points receives a prize. You may want to plan different events to which you can invite people from school. There may even be some things at your school that your youth group can do. If you need money that you don't have to accomplish some of the things in your plan, don't give up. Just plan some fundraisers, do some car washes or whatever you can do. Remember there is always a way and it can be done. We must adopt this attitude.

There are also many materials that are already created to help

this generation needs a lot more than a gentle nudge toward the Lord. they need a jolt from God that will transform their lives

you in this process. I have written a book called *Revolution YM: The Complete Guide to High-Impact Youth Ministry*, which comes with a CD-ROM, that details a step-by-step process of how to dynamically grow your youth ministry in size and impact. I have heard story after story of people who have applied the principles in this book and seen their youth group double and even triple in a year. You can order this and other materials in the online store at **http://resources.battlecry.com**. Such materials are available to help you so you don't have to think everything up on your own.

Another great way to get started, especially if your youth group is small, is to partner with other groups. See if there are other churches in the area that you can partner with or join them for big events that you can bring people to. Go to all the Christian clubs at your school to find out what they have going on. Talk to the students there. If they don't have a youth group, invite them to help build yours. Either way, tell everyone in the group about this BattleCry book and see who is interested in developing a battle plan for your school.

Get them to events that will capture their hearts. There is something powerful about getting a person out of their normal environment, away from the everyday distractions, to a event that involves thousands of people who love God. I have seen it weekend after weekend where young people who have just been going through the motions with God, or maybe not even knowing Him at all, come to an Acquire the Fire weekend. Once they are there, God captures their heart and they are never the same again.

This generation needs a lot more than a gentle nudge toward the Lord. They need a jolt from God that will transform their lives. That is why Acquire the Fire was created. Each year it is our goal to bring the latest and best in technology, speakers, and bands to ignite people's hearts to live entirely for God while they are young. We also have several stadium events that are geared specifically to

Sound This Battle Cry to Your Generation. At these events, tens of thousands of young people, just like you, are coming together in defense of their generation to draw a line in the sand and commit to fight for their generation. You can find out about these events at **www.battlecry.com**.

Plug into the army. Just like in a real war, no one fights alone. **www.battlecry.com** will be a central hub where other warriors like yourself can log on to share ideas, be encouraged, and encourage others in the fight. We will also keep you up to date with topics pertaining to the media, your generation, and the Battlecry movement. Think of this as home base when you can meet with other soldiers as you fight together in this battle.

infect the adults in your life with a heart for your generation

Too often what happens in youth ministry is that a bunch of young people get fired up for something and all the adults in the church say, "Isn't that cute" and ignore it. We're not talking about small change here—we are talking about a major U-turn of the largest generation in American history. If we are going to be successful, it is going to take everyone, young and old. Getting the hearts of parents and adults moved for your generation will be crucial if we are going to see any sort of large-scale success.

It's not enough just to reach out to your friends. We must find a way to capture the hearts of the parents and adults as well. I recently heard of a young person who returned from a Global Expeditions mission trip this summer. He came home and set up a meeting with all his supporters to tell them about his trip. After he told them about what happened, he used the rest of his time with them to tell them about the Battlecry movement. As he spoke, their hearts began to awaken to the needs of this young generation. This is the type of dedication it is going to take.

You may want to start by talking to your parents. Encourage them, and every other adult you can, to read through the *Battle Cry for a Generation* book. This will help them better understand the crisis and know how to be involved. You may want to talk to your pastor and ask him if you can share a little bit about what is going on with the church. That way, more parents can be aware and know how to get more information if they would like. There is even a sermon outline at **www.battlecry.com** so your pastor can dedicate a Sunday to informing the adults in the church about the need to reach America's youth.

If we can reach the hearts of adults, they have the influences and the resources to make a huge difference. If we are going to win it is going to take all of us, young and old alike.

advance through the ranks

When you join the military no one wants to stay a private. Your goal is to get your assignment and do it faithfully so that you can move up the ranks where you will be trusted with more and more responsibility and will be able to have a greater impact.

The same is true with the kingdom of God. As we continue to prove faithful in the small things, God will trust us with more. As He continues to trust us with more, we will have opportunities to have greater and greater impact in the world.

The assignments I have laid before you for this next year are just the beginning. These are your first assignments, but make sure you don't stop there. After you lead 7 people to the Lord this year, you will have a lot more experience and be better prepared to win others. So next year, try to double it and reach and disciple 14 people. If your youth group goes from 20 to 40 this year, don't slowdown. Double it again. As you continue to step out in faith with God, you will continue to learn and gain experience that will allow God to promote you to greater responsibility.

It is also important to understand that finding your assignment is not optional. There is no one in the entire army who does not have a task that they are actively working on everyday. So don't think it would be any different in God's army. Most young people have been trained to think that, as long as you are going to church and youth group, you are doing well as a Christian. How ridiculous! How many of you think that a soldier would be doing their duty if they went to a strategy meeting twice a week, but never actually did anything? It would never happen. Every soldier is expected to faithfully engage themselves in their commander-assigned task everyday. As they succeed, they advance through the ranks. It is the same for us. Again, please understand that finding and serving in your assignment from God is not merely a suggestion. It is something every true follower of Christ *must* do. And as you serve faithfully God will continue to give you larger and larger assignments.

I don't know about you but when we all get to heaven, I want to be one of God's generals. I want to be able to talk with Paul and David and Moses. But I don't just want to hear their stories. When they ask me, "Ron, tell us your story. Tell us of the battles you fought for the Lord," I want to have lots of stories to tell them. I want to get to the end of my life and be able to say, like Paul, "I have fought the good fight, I have finished the race, I have kept the faith" (2 Tim. 4:7). For this to be a reality it means we must continually press on for Christ with the reckless abandon of a warrior.

We must never settle, but always desire to accomplish more as effective warriors for God.

CHAPTER NINE

a warrior fights until the battle is won

Many times as Christians, we can get pumped up emotionally, but then drop the ball when it comes to following through. We feel deeply, but keep playing in puddles. Maybe you've been to a Christian camp or retreat when God began to move on your heart. With deep emotion, you made some significant decisions about your life. But when the fire fades, you discover you've lost the desire to execute those decisions. Many times this happens when we get excited about something, but fail to count the cost. In Luke 14:28–30 Jesus says, "Don't begin until you count the cost. For who would begin construction of a building without first getting estimates and then checking to see if there is enough money to pay the bills? Otherwise, you might complete only the foundation before running out of funds. And then how everyone would laugh at you! They would say, 'There's the person who started that building and ran out of money before it was finished!'" (NLT).

In this passage, Jesus is trying to warn people about deciding to follow Him without taking a hard look at the price. Jesus was never, ever unclear with his disciples about what He expected of them. Jesus explained the construction analogy with these words: "No one can become my disciple without giving up everything for me." (Luke 14:33 NLT) That must be the warriors attitude; I will follow orders no matter what it costs me. Perhaps as you've been reading this book, something has been stirring inside of you. As soon as you've read the last page, you plan to run right to the battle. That's good. God is moving in your heart and drawing you to be a part of His plan.

But it's important for all of us to realize we will not win if each us only makes a 10-day commitment. We cannot afford to get all fired-up, only to back down when things get tough. We must count the cost in advance and then be willing to fight until the battle is won.

Going back to our example of an enlisted soldier, it only makes sense. It's unthinkable that a solider would quit before the fighting is over. When our country goes to war, it is expected that soldiers will fight until the mission is completed. The soldiers involved in the battle counted the cost before they ever signed up. They knew what would be expected of them. When it came time to put their lives on the line, they had already made up their minds that they would fight until the end.

If we are going to be warriors for God, we cannot quit until the battle is over.

Throughout this book I have used the terms soldier, warrior, and battle so that you fully understand the level of commitment that we must have as true disciples of Christ. I'm afraid that many have had their view of discipleship ruined by youth leaders who have said (or implied) that a casual commitment to Christ is acceptable . . . that it's okay to "believe" in Jesus without acknowledging His Lordship over their lives. While they may know He is real, they're not experiencing the life-changing effects of His Sovereignty that comes as we offer our lives entirely to Him.

In this chapter I want to make absolutely sure you have a clear definition of what a follower of Christ looks like. Based on what Jesus taught us about following Him, consider the following points a checklist for your life:

devotion

We live in a society that does not know much of devotion anymore. Marriage used to be a shining symbol of unquestioning loyalty to another individual. But these days, even in the sacred covenant of marriage, which was designed to be a lifelong commitment, is held in low regard. In fact, many people today are actually changing their vows to reflect a lower commitment level. The traditional vows of marriage end with the famous words, "until death do us part." Now people are replacing that last line with words to the effect: "as long as our love shall last." Is that incredible or what?! As a result, half of all marriages in America end in divorce (even among church-going folks). Where is the commitment? Where is the devotion?

Imagine standing at the altar with your future spouse-to-be. The person promises to love you and cherish you, through good times and bad, be faithful to you, all these nice things. But after each promise, your spouse-to-be adds this qualifier: "for as long as

I still love you." How good would you feel about that commitment? A relationship like that would be doomed from the start. Everyone knows that in marriage there are good times and bad times, easy times and hard times. But only as you stick it out with that person, in a spirit of devotion through all of those seasons, does your relationship with that person become rewarding and fulfilling beyond words.

The Bible often describes God's relationship to His people in marriage terms. And so it should be no surprise that many times our relationship with the Lord can fall into the same trap that marriages fall into—except God is never "contributing to the problem." It's always us.

Like marriage, we must commit ourselves to Christ for life. No matter what obstacles, pain, or losses that you face, you must promise to stay faithful to Christ through it all. Too many of us have taken the "as long as my love shall last" approach to our relationship with Christ. We may come to the altar with fiery emotions and sincere intentions, fully ready to obey the Lord no matter what. But then as soon as some peer pressure hits or a little temptation arrives, we cave in. We become unfaithful to the One we have committed to serve. There are many, many Christians today, both young and old, who are caught in the cycle of falling away and repenting, and falling away and repenting. If that's the case, I wonder if they ever really took the time to count the cost before making a commitment to Christ.

The biggest problem of getting sucked into this downward spiral is that you never make any progress in your relationship with God. People in this pattern spend most their time getting back to square one, only to move two steps forward, and three steps back. What we're called to do is to steadily move forward and advance into the enemy's territory. We're talking about taking spiritual ground for Christ. If we are going to do significant battle with the enemy, it will require a level of devotion that we must commit to *in advance* if we're going to have what we need for the long haul.

A great example of devotion comes from the famous story called "The Count of Monte Cristo." Edmond Dantes is a man who is wrongfully accused and imprisoned on a remote island. After many, many years he is able to escape and ends up running into a band of pirates. The pirate captain, Luigi, informs Edmond that he has appeared at a very fortunate time. Apparently one of their crew members, Jacopo, had been caught stealing from the bounty. Apparently the last thing you want to do, if you're a pirate, is to steal from other pirates. So, the captain brought Jacapo to this island to bury him alive for his crime. However, the captain tells Edward that some on the crew wants to see Jacapo spared. This presented the corrupt captain with a problem. If he were to show mercy to Jacopo, he may appear soft and lose control of the crew. But if the captain just kills him, he may lose the loyalty of Jacopo's friends. So the captain will allow Edmond and the thief to fight to the death. That way if Jacopo wins, he has not been too soft and those who wanted him back will be thankful. If Jacopo loses, then those who wanted to see Jacopo spared won't complain because he was at least given a chance. Edmond reluctantly enters the fight, and gains a decisive advantage over the thief. However instead of killing Jacopo, he tells the captain that there's a better solution. Jacopo has suffered enough at the prospect of being killed. The men have seen some sport and know that the captain is not a pushover. By keeping *both* of them alive, he will have an additional person on his crew.

This seems like a good idea to the captain and the rest of the crew. After realizing that Edmond has just saved his life, Jacopo pulls him close and swears to him: "I am your man forever." He dedicated his life to Edward out of gratitude. Jacopo spends the rest of the story faithfully serving the one who saved his life—no matter what the circumstances.

What a great example of unconditional devotion that comes from gratefulness! And this should be our response to Christ. He ransomed us from certain death and gave us new life. Surely He deserves the totality of our devotion.

There's another famous story of a captain who led his troops to a far away land by way of the sea. After the troops left the ship, the captain had the boats burned. When his warriors saw this, they knew there was no way they were going back. The only direction they could go was forward—and straight toward the enemy. Retreating was no longer an option, even if the fighting got fierce. By eliminating their only route of escape, the commanding officer ensured that his troops would fight with wholehearted devotion—because there was no alternative to victory.

Guess what? They won.

This is the type of no-retreat mentality God calls us to. We might have to take a break once in awhile, so we can get reenergized. But those times of rest must always be temporary. We can never settle for "the couch," just watching the game from a distance. If we are followers of Christ, we must fully engage and decide that there will be no turning back. We must count the cost in advance, knowing there will be fun times and not-so-fun times. There will be times when we don't feel like doing what we know we must do. There will be times where peers may respond to what

Photo © Photodisc

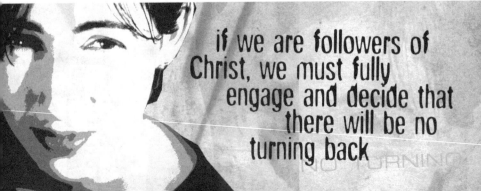

if we are followers of Christ, we must fully engage and decide that there will be no turning back

we believe with sarcasm. But you'll see; it's a small price to pay. Once you've crossed the line of full devotion to Christ, suddenly a lot of life's decisions are much easier to make. Doesn't Christ deserve our wholehearted devotion, no matter how hard it gets? Those who will respond with devotion, after counting the cost, are the type of warriors God needs to win this war.

defiance

Maybe you have heard the term *defiance* before. Chances are you have heard it used to describe something negative—like when children are "defiant" to their parents. The word *defiance* actually means to boldly resist an authority or an opposing force. Almost every teenager has had experience with that at one time or another. While you may have expressed this in a bad way or directed it at the wrong person or authority, you can use this defiance in a way that actually honors God!

In order to win this battle we must have warriors who are willing to defiantly resist the enemy. There is a certain attitude we must have that says, "I will not be deceived. I am tired of having my life and the lives of my friends ruined by the devil. There is no way I am going to let him conquer me or anybody else I know for that matter. I refuse to be ruled or held in bondage by Satan or any other demonic force or ideology!"

God is looking for people that are willing to stand in defiance of the enemy and forcefully advance the kingdom of God (see Matthew 11:12). Many nations have been inhabited by people who were being oppressed by those ruling over them. Some of them finally stood up for themselves and said enough is enough. We are going to fight for our freedom. That's the reason the United States exists today.

In the same way there will be a revolution in your generation when you and your friends (and thousands you may not know until heaven) begin to have that attitude that says to the world: we're not going to take anymore. It's time for the young men and women of God to rise up with defiance against the enemy and say, "I'm done with you. I won't be deceived anymore! We're tired of the devil oppressing us and destroying our generation. We are going to stand up, and with holy defiance, defeat the devil as a united army of God!"

David had this same defiant attitude when he fought Goliath. The six-fingered giant was intimidating the Israelites. He would walk out to the middle of the battlefield everyday and mock the armies of Israel . . . and God! Israel's soldiers would retreat and cower in fear when they heard the too-tall Philistine. David arrived on the battlefield to bring some supplies to his brothers, but when he found out what this Philistine was doing, he became livid. Something stirred up inside of him: an attitude of defiance against an enemy who had no regard for God or those who belonged to Him. David said, "Who is this uncircumcised Philistine that he should defy the armies of the living God?" (1 Sam. 17:26). David's defiance, combined with courageous faith, compelled the young man to take Goliath's challenge. Guess who won? God is still looking for young people like David today who will stand in defiance against the devil.

Sometimes I talk to young people who want to serve the Lord, but they are constantly giving in to sin. That's not an attitude of defiance. That's like someone who knows that their enemy will use temptation to attack and destroy them, but they just give in to the bondage and voluntarily become prisoners of war. If we are going to win this battle, we need warriors who develop a righteous hatred for sin. You need to pray that God will make you utterly defiant against the enemy. So, when the devil tries to tempt you, you won't flirt with sin or get enticed by his deception. Instead you will see right through it. When you get tempted (and you will), you'll get mad because you know he's trying to use these things to ruin your life.

If we are going to stay in the fight for its duration, we must ask God to give us an attitude of defiance toward the enemy.

courage

Fighting until the battle is won is also going to take uncommon courage. When you read the Bible, you see example after example of God doing great things through people who had courage. As we talked about, God used David (the disrespected "baby" of the family) to take care of Goliath. God used an insecure guy like Gideon to lead 300 troops against an army of over 100,000. God used Moses (who didn't like speaking in public) to lead millions of people out of bondage. The common ingredient in all these Bible stories was courage—despite any flaws in their characters.

Maybe you've thought, *I want God to use me to do great things like that.* Well then, I've got some good news for you. God will use you to do great things, but you will need to have some courage. Would you be willing to stand up against someone that was 9 feet tall with nothing more than a sling shot—like David did? That would take some serious courage. While it's true there are not a lot of ugly giants running around, courage is just as necessary. There may never be a physical giant in front of you. But your fear may seem 9 feet tall when God is calling you to witness to someone you wouldn't normally talk to.

You see when God did great things through people they always had to step out in faith. That takes courage. For example, David needed courage to step out in faith against Goliath. Moses needed courage when he had the Red Sea in front of him and the Egyptian army behind him. Gideon needed courage when he had to send all but 300 of his soldiers home even though they were about to face a great army. Often times God wants to do great things through us, but we lack the guts. God is still looking for people like David and Gideon and Moses who will step up to the plate, despite their fears, in order to make a difference for Him.

Ever wonder where David got the nerve to stand up and take on a giant like Goliath? Saul, the king of Israel at the time, wondered the same thing. When the older man questioned him David replied, "Your servant has killed both the lion and the bear; this uncircumcised Philistine will be like one of them..." (1 Sam. 17:36). David found courage by looking to the past, and remembering when God had delivered him. David developed a lifestyle threaded with courage. When he was a shepherd and predators threatened his flock, he'd charge them and kill them. As he passed these small tests of courage, God gave him bigger and bigger ones.

In what area of life is God asking you to live more courageously? Are you living with courage when it comes to obeying the Lord in your personal life? Are you displaying the courage to not let the world shape you in the type of things that you see, listen to, wear, and say? Are you exercising courage when you have the opportunity to make a stand for Christ in the face of negative peer pressure? God can develop great courage in you like He did with David, but it will not just come out of thin air. You must start living with courage now in the seemingly-small opportunities God places in your path.

Courage is never optional in a time of war. Those who succumb to their fears will only get crushed. Courage is mandatory for the warrior. Courage does not mean you are fearless; it means you're willing to move through your fear. Despite whatever you're afraid of, you will do what you know God wants you to do. We must

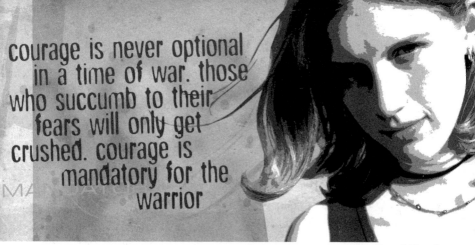

courage is never optional in a time of war. those who succumb to their fears will only get crushed. courage is mandatory for the warrior

Photo © Photodisc

prepare our hearts *in advance* so that when courage is needed, we won't back down. The devil will not let go of you or the rest of your generation without a vicious fight. As He has done throughout history, God is still looking for heroes. And the primary characteristic of God's heroes is courage.

endurance

Courage exercised over the long haul develops into endurance. Maybe you've had an experience like this: You go to a prayer meeting, and decide you are going to reach out to people. You wholeheartedly agree with the decision. Up to that point, you have not been talking to people like you need to. But now all that is going to change (you say to yourself). Armed with your newfound courage, you set out. The next day you pass someone in the halls of your school, and you feel the Holy Spirit tug on your heart to show them Christ's love. You respond with obedience and courage, and begin a conversation with that person. Eventually the 2 of you start talking about Jesus, But that person doesn't respond in the way you were hoping. There doesn't seem to be any immediate fruit. You walk away from the conversation feeling defeated. The bubble has burst. Your newfound courage has evaporated, and you begin

to entertain thoughts from the enemy about how hard it is to identify with Christ. Sound familiar?

This is a classic example of having courage without
endurance. While courage is crucial as we just discussed, the
battle is not going to be won overnight. We're in a marathon, not a
40-yard dash, so to our courage we must add endurance.

Timothy (in the New Testament) sets a high standard as a role
model. He was young, probably only an older teen, when Paul left
him to pastor a church! Timothy had already traveled with Paul, his
mentor, and had proven that he was faithful. So Paul gave Timothy
some critical advice as they were establishing the church during
this crucial time in history.

- Endure hardship with us like a good soldier of Christ
  Jesus (2 Timothy 2:3).
- This is why I remind you to fan into flames the
  spiritual gift God gave you when I laid my hands on you
  (2 Timothy 1:6 NLT).
- But you should keep a clear mind in every situation. Don't
  be afraid of suffering for the Lord. Work at bringing others
  to Christ. Complete the ministry God has given you
  (2 Timothy 4:5 NLT).

As Timothy was serving the Lord, and doing great things for
God, there were many difficult things that he had to face. Apparently
there were hardships and even suffering at times that Timothy had

as you decide to fight for our God with
devotion, defiance, courage, and
endurance—you'll have everything it
takes to become one of God's heroes

to endure. So Paul encouraged him to fan into flames his spiritual gifts. Timothy was probably tired and Paul was reminding him to keep his hope alive and to not stop doing God's work.

As you serve God throughout your life, it will not always be fun and games. Just like any war, there will be times of hardship and struggle where endurance is needed. There will be times when you may have to endure some personal turmoil while God is changing you. You may have to endure persecution for the stand you are taking for Christ. You may have to endure disappointment as those you are discipling seem to make little progress. You will have to endure the attacks of the enemy as he becomes more and more irritated with you and the damage you are doing to his ever-shrinking kingdom.

While fighting in God's army will be difficult at times, I want to ask you a question. What is the alternative? We either serve God with endurance, fight until the battle is won, and then stand before God at the end of our lives as a successful soldier. Or we can quit, sit on the sidelines, live as a half-hearted Christian, and then have to answer to God for not using the talents and gifts He gave us. Seems like Option #2 isn't that great. It's not that I don't ever get tired or trials never come my way. They come all the time. But with each new trial, I remind myself that quitting is not an option. Sure it may be easier to quit, but then a generation will not be reached. I'll be letting down the one person who gave His life for me.

I don't want to do that.

Keep in mind that we are talking about endurance—not perfection. I talk to a lot of young people who feel like they have failed God because they've made mistakes along the way. Some mistakes are sinful, but many of them are not. In any case, the enemy loves to use those failures to make these kids feel disqualified from the fight. Endurance doesn't mean you live mistake-free; it's about never quitting. If I sin, I repent and move forward in God's grace and forgiveness. And I make non-sinful mistakes all the time. But each time, I try to learn from the experience, get back up, and keep fighting. I stay in the battle to get closer to Christ and to persevere for His kingdom. The devil isn't afraid of your perfection—that's a lost cause no matter how good you think you are. What he fears most is your endurance, because he knows if you hang in there by the power of God, you'll eventually win.

As you decide to fight the long fight, God will begin to fashion the heart of a warrior in you. Guy or girl, young or old, God will transform your heart into one that will not be stopped in its pursuit, slowed in its progress, or denied victory. As you decide to fight for our God with devotion, defiance, courage, and endurance—you'll have everything it takes to become one of God's heroes.

If we are going to be true disciples of Christ, it is mandatory that we arm ourselves with devotion, defiance, courage, endurance, and a desire to continue advancing the kingdom of God.

Dear God, right now, in this moment, I know what it's going to cost me to serve You: everything. I know that it will not be easy. I know that there will be times of great joy and times of great loss. But in spite of whatever comes my way, I commit to live for You with devotion, defiance, courage, and endurance. Give me the heart of a warrior who will never stop or slow down in my pursuit of You and Your purposes through me. When You come again, I want to be considered one of Your heroes.

In Jesus' name. Amen.

CHAPTER TEN

making history

divine opportunities

From time to time throughout history, there have been special opportunities that have fallen into the laps of certain generations. These opportunities were so large they shaped the course of human history. These were not opportunities that were chosen, asked for, or even avoided. They simply came to those whom God has picked.

What they did with the opportunity determined the course of human history.

There were several such turning points in our own nation. The first was the generation that fought for the independence of what we now call the United States of America. This generation was tired of oppression and the lack of religious freedom that held their people in bondage. Out of their devotion, righteous defiance, and courage, the most powerful nation in the world was born.

Then there was the generation who fought through the Civil War. A dispute arose over racial equality that threatened to split our country into two nations. Again, a generation rose to the occasion and our nation was preserved.

Can you imagine how different the world would be today if our country was fragmented into different countries? We may have split even further in the succeeding years, and, today, we would not look much different from Europe.

The World War II generation that we spoke of earlier probably would not exist. Those from our country who were in involved in WWII did not purposely seek out a history-shaping opportunity—it just happened. They could not avoid it; they either needed to respond, or be consumed. The impact of this generation's sacrifice on the history of the world is immeasurable.

When it comes to the advancement of the Gospel, there are also significant opportunities that fall to certain generations. Occasions that will not only affect the course of history, but all of eternity. I want to share one such example with you because it reminds me of the opportunity that lies before you right now.

In the late 1200s, the uncle and father of the famous explorer, Marco Polo, were visiting what we know today as China (and some of it's surrounding regions). The Polo brothers met with the ruler of the region, Kublai Khan, who was the grandson of the famous ruler Genghis Khan. During their visit they told him many things about the western world, including Christianity. Kublai expressed so much interest in the claims of Christ that he sent letters back with the Polo brothers asking the pope to send 100 missionaries who could tell him and his people more about the Christian faith. He went on to say that if they could simply show him why the Christian faith was truer than all other religions of the world, then he and all his followers would commit their lives to Christ. When the Polo brothers eventually delivered the letters to the pope, he had other more pressing matters on his mind. Instead of sending the 100 missionaries, he sent only 2 Dominican monks—who unfortunately turned back in fear for their lives.

When you look at the territory that the Khan oversaw, it is much of what we know today as the 10/40 window. The 10/40 window refers to the least-evangelized area of the world. Since the time of Kublai Khan, billions of people have lived and died in that region without ever even hearing the name of Jesus. What would have happened if those 100 missionaries had been sent? What if even one of them was able to lead Kublai to Christ and through him, his entire nation came to know the Lord? Perhaps the 10/40 would today would be known as one of the *most* evangelized regions in the world. How many hundreds of millions, if not billions of people would be in heaven today if that opportunity had been handled differently? We will never know, but it will go down as one of the greatest missed opportunities for the advancement of the Gospel in the history of the world.

We are facing such an opportunity again with your generation. How you and your believing peers rise to this occasion is going to shape the next 50 to 100 years of American history. No kidding. You will also be able to shape the kind of influence America has on the rest of the world over that period of time.

The potential impact is staggering.

You may be thinking, "I don't want that type of responsibility" or "why me?" While those are valid questions, the fact of the matter is that you have been chosen to fight on one of the greatest spiritual battlegrounds in history. You cannot avoid it, or escape from it. Like Jonah, it won't matter how hard you try to run in the other direction, you will end up in the place God intends for you. What you do there is up to you. How will you respond? Will you rise to the occasion, put your hand to the plow, to rescue your generation? Are you willing to throw yourself into a battle that will change the world?

God has chosen you to be a part of this generation for such a time as this. He has allowed this book to fall in your hands as an invitation to the battle. God is looking for warriors who will fight for Him on the battlefield of minds and hearts. He's handing the torch over to you so that shines brightly in our nation—not just for you, but for your children and for future generations.

beyond the battle

As you finish this book I want to leave you with one final reminder. There is a day coming when every battle—physical and spiritual—will come to an end. That's the day when the King of kings and the Lord of lords, Jesus Christ, returns to this earth. On that day all of mankind will be called to give an account of our lives to the Lord. Do your best to picture that moment in your mind, standing before the Lord to answer for your life. This will be the most important day in the rest of your existence. Live every hour with that great day in mind. On that day nothing else will matter. Every trivial distraction that sidetracked you will seem so foolish.

Photo © Photodisc

God has chosen you to be a part of this generation for such a time as this

Many will wish they could have the wasted moments of their lives back, so they could live them over again in a way that would count for eternity. But it will be too late to go back.

But there's no reason to fear that this has to happen to you. God has given us a heads up. The Day is coming, so don't waste your life. God has given such an incredible opportunity to your generation. But with very opportunity comes accountability. Each of us will be called to answer to the Lord for how we handled the chances He gave to us. Don't get distracted by lesser things and empty promises. Don't stay blind to the battles raging around you. Live each day wholeheartedly for God so that you will not be unprepared for when Christ returns. Instead, decide to live so that you can say, like the Apostle Paul, "I fought the good fight."

it's time to fight

My prayer is that this generation will rise up and change the course of history. I pray that the 4 percent of Bible-believing Christians that are projected for this generation will grow to 14 percent and then 24 percent and then 34 percent and then 44 percent. It may seem like a big task, but Jesus reminds us that "with God, all things are possible" (Matt. 19:26).

You are standing on the edge of the one of the greatest spiritual battlefields in history. A generation, your generation, is hanging in the balance. But I can see an army rising. Thousands . . . tens of thousands . . . hundreds of thousands . . . *millions* from your generation who are rising up to stand against the enemy. They are those who have enlisted their lives into God's army and are gathering for the fight of the ages.

Are you ready to run to the battle?

Yes, I'm Enlisted!

This is your chance to make a serious, no-compromise commitment to fighting the battle for Christ. Check each action step that you are committed to.

☑ **Enlist**. I am a warrior in the army of God. I let go of any claim on my life. I submit my life to Christ and am born-again through Him.

☑ **Devote**. I am totally and completely devoted to Jesus Christ, my Master and Commander. I love Him passionately and will follow Him every day, no matter the cost.

☑ **Defy**. I will live in defiance of Satan's tactics. I will see through the world's lies, hate what is evil, and cling to what is good (Rom. 12:9).

☑ **Be Courageous**. No matter what it costs, I will stand up courageously for God's Truth every day.

☑ **Endure**. I don't care how long, how exhausting, or how painful the fight becomes, I am in it for the long haul.

☑ **Advance**. I will not remain a private in God's army but will grow in faith and maturity as I study the Word and go to church. I will advance through the ranks.

☑ **Multiply**. I will reach and disciple 7 of my peers this year. I understand that being a warrior means I will draw others to God and help them grow as His disciples.

☑ **Double the Size of My Youth Group Every Year**. I will talk to my youth pastor and my friends about the battle. I will make it a visible, public part of my life and get my peers involved in a thriving youth ministry.

☑ **Recruit Adults**. I will help adults catch a heart for my generation and understand the urgency of the battle. I will do whatever it takes to get adults committed to reaching out to young people, whether it's getting adults to read *Battle Cry for a Generation* to talking with my head pastor or elder board.

By signing this page, you are pledging to be a warrior for Christ, regardless of the dangers, challenges, or temptations that may come.
You are committed!

_____   8/30/06
signature   date

END NOTES

1 Associated Press, "Update 2:Viacom 2Q Results Rise on Cable,TV" on the Web at www.Forbes.com /07/22/04, 10:47 AM.

2 U.S.Census Bureau.

3 Thom S.Rainer, The Bridger Generation:America's Second Largest Generation, What They Believe, How to Reach Them (Nashville, TN: Broadman & Holman Publishers, 1997).

4 Research Shows That Spiritual Maturity Process Should Start at a Young Age, The Barna Group,Ltd., November 17,2003. http://www.barna.org/FlexPage.aspx?Page=Barna Update&BarnaUpdateID=153.

5 To find statistics like these—and many others—go to such Web sites as: www.parentstv.org; www.frc.org; or www.clickz.com/stats/sectors/demographics.

6 For information about the most influential writers/producers, see:"Violence and Promiscuity Set the Stage for Television's Moral Collapse," Issue #: 248 www.frc.org/get.cfm?i=IS02E4.

7 Time Magazine, "Video Vigilantes," January 10,2005.

8 Reported by Rob McGann in an article titled, "Internet Edges Out Family Time More than TV Time," January 5, 2005, at Web site: www.clickz.com/stats/sectors/demographics/article.php/3455061.

9 Regarding the amount of porn sites and spam, see: National Coalition for the Protection of Children & Families www.nationalcoalition.org/internet porn/internetporn.html.

10 For statistics on how much television children are watching, see: http://www.tvturnoff.org/images/facts&figs/factsheets/FactsFigs.pdf.

11 Parent TV Council, p.4

12 See pages 22-23 of Report 6 article. Footnoted in that article to Family Pride Canada, Web site: http://familypride.uwo.ca/teens/teenbk2.html.

13 "Violent Videogames a Case for Legislation," by Valerie Smith. Submitted to the Canadian Association of Chiefs of Police and the Canadian Police Association, March 13,2003.

14 "Violent Videogames a Case for Legislation," Ibid.

15 "Violent Videogames a Case for Legislation," Ibid.

16 "Monkey See, Monkey Do," p.6 (Associated Press, 5/14/02).

17 "Monkey See, Monkey Do," p.7 (BBC News Online, 7/13/01).

18 From a news story on CNN.com, "Lawsuit filed against Sony,Wal-Mart over game linked to shootings," 10/23/03.

19 "Pornography Targets the Teenage Brain, Mind, Memory and Behavior: America's Children versus the Impotence Industry." Report prepared by Judith A. Reisman, Ph.D., the Institute for Media Education.

20 "Pornography Targets the Teenage Brain, Mind, Memory and Behavior: America's Children versus the Impotence Industry," Ibid.

21 Alan Guttmacher Institute ,"Patterns of Contraception Use Within Teenagers'First Sexual Relationships," CPYU's Youth Culture e-Update #51, 1/14/04.

22 J. Mitchell Kimberly, et.al., The exposure of youth to unwanted sexual material on the Internet. Youth & Society, Vol. 34 no.3, March 2003, pp.330-358.

23 Judith Reisman, Soft Porn Plays Hard Ball: Its Tragic Effects on Women, Children and the Family (Lafayette, LA: Huntington House, 1991.

24 "Pornography Statistics 2003," Family Safe Media.

25 "Pornography Statistics 2003," Ibid.

26 Speech by Judith Reisman given at a Science, Technology, and Space Hearing: "The Science Behind Pornography Addiction," Thursday, November 18, 2004. Available on the Web at: http://commerce.senate.gov/hearings/testimony. cfm?id=1343&wit_id=3910.

27 See drjudithreisman.org, White papers on the FBI and DOJ reduction of child sexual abuse reports for the GOA study on sex-offender treatment failure studies.

28 Testimony for U.S. Senate Committee on Commerce, Science, and Transportation, November 18, 2004, by Mary Anne Layden, Ph.D., Co-Director Sexual Trauma and Psychopathology Program. She is also director of the Education Center for Cognitive Therapy, the Department of Psychiatry, at the University of Pennsylvania.

29 Reisman,"The Science Behind Pornography Addiction," Op.Cit.

30 "Gateway Drugs," by A.J. Czerwinskia. Available on the Web at
    http://www.goerie.com/niegatewaytab/gateway_drugs.html.

31 Child Trends Data Bank, "Substance Free Youth," 6/8/04.

32 William J. Bennett, quoted in an article by Jim Fredricks, "Cat in the Hat," Houston Community
    Newspapers Online, 12/10/03. Available on the Web at:
    www.hcnonline.com/site/news.cfm?BRD=1574&dept_id=532225&newsid=10607974&PAG=461&rfi=9.

33 Quoted from the Commercial Closet, a gay-oriented Web site at http://www.commercialcloset.org/cgi-
    bin/iowa/portrayals.html? record=719.

34 Statistics from the Heritage Foundation Web site in a footnoted article, "Sexually Active Teenagers Are
    More Likely to Be Depressed and to Attempt Suicide," by Robert E.Rector, Kirk A. Johnson, and Lauren
    R.Noyes, Center for Data Analysis Report #03-04. June 3,2003.
    http://www.heritage.org/Research/Family/cda0304.cfm#_ftn1.

35 Chap Clark, Hurt: Inside the World of Today's Teenagers (Grand Rapids, MI: Baker Academic, 2004), p.123.

36 A.R.Luria in Daniel Goleman and Richard Davidson, Eds., Consciousness, Brain, States of Awareness, and
    Mysticism. Harper & Row, New York, 1979, at 10.

37 Pasko Rakic, Science, Vol 294, "Enhanced: Neurocreationism—Making New Cortical Maps," November
    2,2001, at 1024-5.

38 Patrick Carnes, Out Of The Shadows:Understanding Sexual Addiction, Minneapolis Minn.: CompCare,
    1983.

39 National Institute of Mental Health (NIMH), Office of Communications and Public Liaison, Email: nimhin-
    fo@nih.gov. Web site: http://www.nimh.nih.gov. Child and adolescent mental health information:
    http://www.nimh.nih.gov/publicat/childmenu.cfm Barlow,Sakheim and Beck, The Journal of Abnormal
    Psychology.

40 Oxytocin is released by genital stimulation in males and females and is implicated in sexual and maternal
    behaviors. Cornell University,
    http://instruct1.cit.cornell.edu/courses/bionb424/students/nzl1/Oxytocin.htm.

41 Peters, op.cit.

42 E.K. Sommers and Check, J.V. Violence and Victims 1987, pp 2:189-209. For full documentation of research
    cited here see, Peter Stock, "The Harmful Effects on Children of Exposure to Pornography," Canadian
    Institute for Education on the Family, November, 2004. http://www.cief.ca/research_reports/harm.htm.

43 M.Allen, and D'Allessio, A meta-analysis summarizing the effects of pornography II: Aggression after
    exposure. Human Communication Research, 1995, pp.22, 258-283.

44 Jennings Bryant, "Report to Attorney General Commission on Pornography," U.S. Dept.of Justice, 1986.

45 C.Everett Koop, "Report of the Surgeon General's Workshop on Pornography and Public Health." American
    Psychologist. 1987 Oct. Vol. 42 (10), pp.944-945.

46 Schimmer,R, "The impact of sexually stimulating materials and group care residents: A question of harm."
    Residential Treatment for Children and Youth, 11, 1993, pp.37-55.

47 Court,J.H. "Sex and violence:a ripple effect." In N.Malamuth and E.Donnerstein,eds., Pornography and
    Sexual Aggression (New York: Academic Press, 1984).

48 The four studies include two by Donnerstein:

•   Edward Donnerstein, "Aggressive Erotica and Violence Against Women." Journal of Personality and Social
    Psychology, Vol.39, No.2, 1980, pp.269-277.

•   Edward Donnerstein, and Berkowitz, L. "Victim reactions in aggressive-erotic films as a factor in violence
    against women." Journal of Personality and Social Psychology, 1981, 41:710724.

•   Neal Malamuth. "Erotica,aggression and perceived appropriateness." Paper presented at the 86th annual
    convention of the American Psychological Association,Toronto,Canada,1978.

•   Jennings Bryant,"Report to Attorney General Commission on Pornography,"U.S.Dept.of Justice,1986.

49 Dolf Zillman and Jennings Bryant,"Pornography's Impact on Sexual Satisfaction."Journal of Applied Social
    Psychology,1988:vol 18,no.5,pp 438-453;and Zillman and Bryant,"Effects of Prolonged Consumption of
    Pornography on Family Values."Journal of Family Issues: vol.9, No.4,Dec.1988,pp 518-544.

50 Charles Colson,"Merchants of Cool,"in Christianity Today,June 11, 2001, Vol. 45, No. 8, p. 112.

Hey, look what's hot . . .
Acquire the Fire
Teen Devozine

Our devozine is a new full-color teen devotional that flips, half for girls and half for guys.

Created just for you, the devozine will help you on your quest for unconditional love—with some fun mixed in! Being real and passionate for the things of God is what we're all about.

Inside you'll find:

- Biblically-sound devotionals in each issue
- Info on the latest Christian bands
- Amazing testimonies

- Super "Top 10" lists and great quizzes
- Articles on the hottest teen topics
- Teen-to-Teen Wisdom
- And much, much more!

Four new issues every year!

To get your copies, visit your favorite bookstore, call 1-800-323-7543, or visit www.battlecry.com.

YOU'VE ENLISTED.

IT'S TIME TO TAKE TO THE BATTLE FIELD AND SAVE YOUR GENERATION!

Talk to your youth leader about *Rise Up: Basic Training for Warriors*, a spiritual boot camp that will get your entire youth group involved in the battle.

Then let *Over the Edge: Extreme Commitment* be your battle guide as you fight against Satan's lies. Over the next seven weeks, you will be challenged to live every day totally sold-out to Christ, your Master and Commander.

Now the battle begins! Working through *Over the Edge: Extreme Commitment* you'll learn to apply specific action steps that will help you become fully equipped to face the demands of the world and succeed as you live for Jesus.

HERE'S WHAT TO EXPECT:

>> **Get a chance to dive deeper into the issues you looked at during *Rise Up: Basic Training for Warriors***
>> **Be invited to dig into the Word every day**
>> **Discover specific strategies for countering the lies that have infiltrated your entertainment, your school, and all the places in between**

Don't let one more day pass—learn to live a life of *Extreme Commitment!*